line of sight

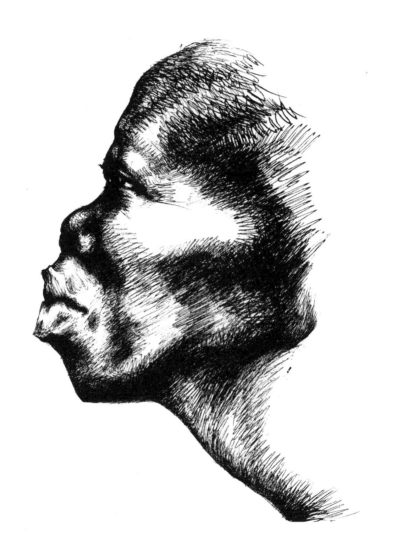

LINE OF SIGHT

Michele D. Gibbs

West End Press

Credits

The poetry in this volume first appeared in the following collections
by Michele D. Gibbs:

Can You Dig It?, Free West Indian Publishing Co., Grenada, West Indies
(1981)

Sketches from Home, Broadside Press, Detroit (1983)

Riffin' to a Maroon Tune, Broadside Press, Detroit (1996)

Otra Onda, From the Field Pubs., Oaxaca, Mexico (2001)

Blows, From the Field Pubs., Oaxaca, Mexico (2004)

The essays in this volume first appeared in the following publications:

"Slave Codes and Liner Notes," in *The Radical Teacher,* March 1977.

"Black-Eyed Blues Connections: From the Inside Out," in *Heresies:
Third World Women's Issue,* 1979.

Both essays were anthologized in *All the Women Are White, All the Blacks Are
Men, but Some of Us Are Brave,* edited by Gloria T. Hull, Patricia Bell Scott,
and Barbara Smith; Feminist Press, 1982.

Cover and interior art by Michele D. Gibbs

First edition July, 2004

West End Press • PO Box 27334 • Albuquerque, New Mexico 87125

Contents

Acknowledgments

To Akasha Gloria Hull, for keeping my early work in print and me in mind over the years; to John Crawford, for adding my trajectory into the body of working class women's writing West End Press has published; to the close friendship network of my sisters too numerous to list in the Caribbean, Mexico, and the United States whose experience is the basis of my expression and whose feedback keeps it all real; and to my parents, Paula Rabinowitz and Ted Gibbs, who gave me the best possible start in life. Thank you.

To Jean ~
and more time to share
all we have in common.

abrazos,
Michele

Oaxaca
Spring, 2007

Michele Gibbs & George Colman
1417 A Jose López Alavez
Barrio de Xochimilco
Oaxaca, OAX. 68040
MÉXICO
tel# 513-4690

prelude

Family Tree

prelude

dese words be wounds
wound round sound;
riddim
de pulse
knitting memory's tissue
into keloid's common weal.

wide de wound,
jagged its trace upon skin.
round de sound,
swollen with all we have lived.

sacred de ground
where seeds of sound
watered with sweat
sprout into song.

we tell the story

westory start where
storm clouds gather;
faith wavers.
ghosts penetrate a continent's interior.
villages shatter.
we are captured / cut up / separated:
the better to feed the slavers' greed.

fire stalks our every move.
salt tears, sweat, middle passage sea
damp down freedom's flame
coat our vision
streak our pain
soak each note we sing.
wring us out
Goree 'door of no return.'

soon,
waves' swell becoming a roll
produced the stroll.
three steps forward / one, back
a motion to slow down the lockstep
then add some bounce:
a rebound to the whip's pounce.

when we finally land
without the many million drowned
our strength
stands on auction block docks: bare.
peopling Congo Square.
stud
mare
beast of burden.
that horse, ridden for show,
better cared for, worth more
to them
than this person.

GOING ONCE /
GOING TWICE /
GOING THREE TIMES . . .
SOLD.

through all these hard knocks
we hummed, strummed, ham-boned:
called our gods in any way we could
short of the outlawed drum.

in the throes of our labor,
while our captors sleep
we congregate
and plot escape
miming a dance
as we create our chance
from cakewalk to boogie / between blows' beats
buck an' winging a riddim
to guide us to freedom.

we called it gut bucket
for string, board, and tub.
the humming of the bass
strumming throb
that the sob
of our living creates.
the pulse
in the bottom
of the belly
full slap up the body
through throat to air.
gut bucket.

we ragtime come
from humble material:
kitchen, wash-house,
plantation outback
leftover salvaged funk
and
the prohibition of the drum.

strings were not considered
by our captors
to be instruments of war.

to the European ear
violins signaled revelry
reverie, courtly promenade, good cheer.

in our hands,
cello, bass, fiddle, bottle-necked guitar
conjured screeching vultures
tearing flesh
clinking locks and melodies to flee
took shape from the sounds we found.
gut bucket.
the beating heart in our throat as we ran.
gut bucket
bruggadung rumble of thunder
prelude to rain
gut bucket
thud of the drops on our skin
gut bucket
the trembling deep within:
gut bucket / gut bucket / gut bucket.

and so we
STOLE AWAY
WADED IN THE WATER
FOLLOWED THE DRINKING GOURD
and
LIFTING EVERY VOICE
fashioned our own anthem.

from country to town
the ground we trod
resounded
to notes bent on hope.
with atonal dissonance
crisscrossing diatonic limits
we scaled the heights.
woodshedding shackles
in the wake of death
blowing hard,
we formed a second line of march.

my people
who once flew
knew root time

pelted and dispelled
by rip-torn pull
of dispersal
grew tangled
transcended sorrow
cleared a path through blood
with laughter
pounding out bright minors
dove deep
for chorded harmonies
screamed of chasms
windswept winters of the spirit
with nothing left but body and breath
we
dreamed the universal
key.
took time
and made it swing.

(even as we hung, we swung)

the course we carved
traced by soul-case
sounding
skin, tree
metal, reed
comb, seed
we extend the line
mark our deeds
find the grooves that feel free
allow utmost audacity
are their own authority
where beat-up meets upbeat
our continuity.

blood-riddim drumpulse
contrapuntal
to ship hold
rock steady lock-up
carried us through.
because we could
store the pain
digest absorb transform
and expel it again

in work-chants' pace
believers' grace
code resistance
in a dance
plait up our heads
with memory's trace
let our selves
be mounted in trance
tight-tuned
become medium.

because
each sensate cell
re/members itself
continually
we story stay embedded
bodily:
la tierra de nuestra memoria
more than blows
forging this density
we
showed our captors
how to move
with the real powers that be.

they may get it
one day
freeing themselves, eventually.

I.

seeds took root on the block

Untitled

Q. & A.

"Where did you come out?"
they say,
speaking of home.
our opening onto life.

Was the doorway
narrow?
sunny?
sooty?
edged in wood or iron?
concrete or clay?
thatch or thorn?
hide or horn?
splint-filled or tongued smooth?
barbed or grooved?
and how did the day dawn from there?

What visions filled us
as we crossed the threshold?

What terrors made us bold?

And what force propels us
as we answer back,
"yo' Mama."

to begin

I am a child
of rent parties
poker
and potato salad nights.
Leadbelly and Bird on the box
steaming tamales on the street
and inside, body heat
the beat of cards slapped down,
bottle caps (the pot) raked in.
a break called,
and dancing set to begin.

of hot debates
and grand reunions
when the Chicago Vets from Spain
would gather at our place
and the great Paul Robeson
would put me on his lap
and the rumble from his laugh
filled me from within.

and the songs:
"Viva la Quince Brigada,"
"Valley of Jarama,"
And "Let My People Go."

of intrusions at all hours
from the Feds.
'cause we were Reds.

of times when the sight of my face
was enough
for bosses to show my mom the gate:
"No niggerlovers here."

So I grew
and knew from early in the thick of it
about barbarity,

the kick officially sanctioned,
the hate we were faced with.
what it meant to have thin skin:
a luxury beyond our condition.
and, above all, the hope
within our circle
warmed in struggle
in love and trouble
reaching out across the rubble
that those like us
with a just cause
would win.

religious instruction:
book of revelations

Learning
came in big bites.
like when around the age of eight
i was stopped
from watching Mahalia Jackson on TV
and loving the music
so not understanding that prohibition,
i asked my mother, "Why?"
So she told me
how my father, when a boy of ten
in Texas
came home from school one day
to find his mother
(a large woman, too)
being raped
by one of the white men she did laundry for
and he couldn't forget
how all she seemed able to do about it
was pray harder
and turn the other cheek.

So that was why he hated religion
(in addition, of course, to that white man)
and why i
couldn't watch Mahalia.

I received this news in silence
and transferred my allegiance
to the blues.

saturday snatch

In the kitchen
at the sink
my mom is washing up
to the tune of "My Man."

She remembers Fannie Bryce in the song,
i see only Lady Day.

Her version is Jewish and sad.
Mine is Black and tragic.
We harmonize,
rolling our eyes
on the terrible parts.

Then our man comes home . . .
"and when he takes us in his arms,
the world is bright, all right."

1955

Bandung
Emmett Till hung
Richard Wright's BLACK POWER
tolled the hour
and
a young black girl, nine,
my age,
took the stage
and won $64,000
to spell
antidisestablishmentarianism—
well!
That was progress.

gut-grounded astrology:
first sign

i was born on April 4th
Muddy Waters, too.
on that night in '46
Carnegie Hall rocked
to the eloquent piano of Mary Lou.
in '68, on the same date
when I was 22
Martin Luther King's heart
was blown apart.

ain't I blue?

i grew
to the groan and shout,
the rocksteady beat
our living ground out,
the gusto negating the rut.
enough
to breathe a song or two
hit a note
in tune with the time
schooled to conclude
however funky the mood
that one voice matters:

be it splattered on a wall
substance oozing down
to soak ground
we found home on
it matters.

if it shatters old beliefs
like rock through glass
letting in pollen-laden air
it matters.

if it clatters up the street
pursued by sirens, boots, clubs,
in retreat and beaten
it still matters.

if it howls in the night
forcing you to wake from dreams
to fight, join it.
it matters.

When one becomes two
and we includes you
the harmony sung
creates a new tongue:
the first sign
of a kind that matters.

business goes on as usual;
or
a day on the bus in Detroit can take ten years

I

Never seen so many folk
with their throats
cut:
scars from razors
knives
broken bottles
the tin can's edge
still walking around
and laughing, too.
Glad to be alive
even though they be jammed like cattle
and just as eager for the chute,
bussing it
a little further down the road.

They come
from the barroom's blackness, the concrete cold.
The midnight shift, getting old.
A crowd of crows
flooding Woodward
flapping
toward the bus's running board.
Bold.

"There are some things
children just shouldn't have to see,"
says Lynne,
stopping her daughter of three
from being pushed against the bulging crotch across from us
its contents about to spill
from a ripping seam.
And I agree,
but add,

"There are some things
we don't even need to be."

Like sick.
Hungry
to the point of preying—
on each other.
So in need
that speed becomes a pill
and 'high'
has nothing to do with the sky.

Shouldn't even be caught like this.
Exposed.
Running from every pore.
Bleeding from every vein.
Constantly in pain.
Conscious it's we
children shouldn't have to see.

There are some things
even we
don't need to be.

II

we wear our flesh like war . . .
—Audre Lorde

Early morning
for black women in Detroit
is the hour of maids, cooks,
drill press operators,
first-period students,
and clerks.
Black and blue.
We emerge with powder thickened into masks
and tools on display:
a purposeful array
boarding the bus.

Our uniforms in place
give us time

to get our selves together
behind them.
Wigs on, lips pursed,
only an occasional eyebrow line gone wild
suggests the turmoil we are schooled to hide.
Girded for work.

By noontime
only those not rushing ride.
On the same line
A backward sister
still in the garb of the evening before
does repair-work in transit
to the next trick.
Everything about her is shaky:
from loose flesh
to the way her platform spikes
hoist
and then propel her
down the aisle to a seat.
The one thing between her
and total collapse
is that she doesn't think of it.
She doesn't have time.
Only her hands
swollen from the effect
of maintaining her high
are steady enough
to apply nail polish
as the bus careens.
But her mind,
not ordering things right,
tells her to choose rouge instead
from her regurgitant pack.
A mess
until the sister next
helps her back on track.

On afternoons
when school gets out
so do the switches,

the three layers of hockey socks
to protect shins
and the tight wraps
to emphasize ass—
the teenage teetering
between flaunt and fear.
On key rings,
whips are in this year.
Most are weighted down with chains,
pierced wherever cartilage allows.
Voluntarily.

By quitting time for the office shift,
Our mood has become:
"I got to get me some thing,
any thing, new, please."
And we ready
to do the commodity dash,
snatching after some ornament
to salvage
from the wreckage of the day.
To convince ourselves of what?
That we are worth something?
That our jobs are?
That our enforced regimen of subordination
can at least buy a trinket
signifying pride?
Another trophy conquered from shame?

Day in, day out
we camouflage and guard ourselves
with weapons for deflecting flack.
Wigs, dyes, skins.
Nails like talons,
wrapped, coated and filed to a point.
Gold-capped teeth
to bite through any substance
with flash.
Tiers of hair in flame:
orange, gold, burning bushes
mirroring the rage within,
signaling a fire zone,
sounding alarm.

A day is too short
to do more
than keep your balance
in the crush of bodies,
shifting gears,
and eyes, everywhere bright,
looking for answers,
just like you.
That, and make contact,
stay in touch,
share spare change,
and remember your own destination.

taproot truths

I am not cold
by nature
but was forced to be that way again
with an anger like dry ice
when I heard my mother
at 72
shot and killed,
her breath
spliced
by an unknown youth
who thought
whatever she resisted giving him
was worth her life.

As he fled
she bled to death
on the walkway to her home
in a manner becoming normal
in the USA today.
He, too lost in soul
to know
what she held fast to
was not property,
but dignity—
hers, and his, too.
Everything he threw away,
like the gun,
in his run for safety.

Only a week before
recovering from a stroke,
she spoke so:
"Oh, you know me, dear.
I'm a survivor."
There was no way
she would go from this earth
of her own free will.
There was too much
still to do.

As a Russian Jew
Her childhood knew life
on the cindered sidewalks
of
Chicago's Halsted Street:
the stopping place for those in flight
from the terror of the Tzarist night.
Then, too, her fight
was for the right to roam free,
finish public school,
fashion for herself
the tools to give the lie
to any who regarded her a fool.

And when, in her teens,
She followed elder sister Lillian's lead
And joined Chicago's
Young Communist League
no word of caution, danger
might her mother, Fannie, plead
that my mom, Paula, would heed.
She knew
what she was made to do.

So, in 1930, too,
when she met my father, Ted,
a Black man from Texas
whose path had led from there
across the nation
to Seattle's docks
where the shock-wave of a general strike
carried him into the Party's ranks,
took him through organizer's school,
and sent him to Chicago
to pool his strength with others
in tbe grueling task
of mobilizing the Depression's unemployed mass.

They found each other in the fray,
when work required holding cops at bay
to stay evictions:
the order of the day for millions
who, then as now,

turned grey
seeing their lives dumped
in the street that way.

1936.
The war in Spain.
and Ted Gibbs
along with uncles, cousins, comrades
enlisted in the Abraham Lincoln Brigade:
three years
in which the women
carried on alone, at home.

The men returned
scarred inside and out;
for the time
unable to rout the Fascist terror
which grew in clout
'til it convulsed the world.

Paula still knew what she was about.
She married Ted
as profits fed the war machine
and Amerikan racism
kept nerves razor-keen.
No matter.
They weren't invincible
but knew no other way to live
than by their principles.
Red-baited, blacklisted
they worked, struggled, loved,
kept faith.
Existed.

By my birth in '46
post-war Amerika
opened a new bag of tricks.
Called 'containment' abroad,
Chicago's version
was the Red Squad.
So livid were police to see we three
together and at liberty
they'd run their cars
right up on the curb

and back us up against the wall
when we refused to be perturbed.

Feds at the door
and cops on the beat:
that was the school
of the streets we knew.
Risk everything, say nothing,
and keep your cool.

Saying little in that Emmett Till time,
my father worked:
electrician, carpenter, plumber, gardener,
cook, breadwinner.
Guardian against the beasts of degradation
beating on our door,
he'd take a storefront
and create a home.
Carve a garden from an alley,
coax grass up through stone,
work his long-limbed artist's fingers
to the bone
so the leavings we were allowed to live in
shone
with the light of love.

He was a painter of scenes,
his life a song
from a soul bound to take a stand,
to say this/ and that/ were wrong
fashioned from a longing to be free.
This legacy he passed on to me.

When, finally, he died,
from too much pressure, grieving,
beatings which never did bend his back
or tan his hide,
Paula continued on her own.
She didn't mind, she said,
being alone.
It gave her time to think.

It was 1960 by then
and my turn to join the fight.

Paula would wink
and say, "You know,
you can get killed that way."
I'd laugh, agree,
and do just what their lives
had taught to me,
buoying me up
and giving me eyes to see
the connections between us
commitment weaves.

Well, she kept going
and I did, too.
For the next twenty years
we saw it through
from Watts to Birmingham,
Detroit, Philadelphia, Viet Nam:
years of uninterrupted war
until I chose a farther shore.

She saw me off,
wished me well
and remained
to battle barbarity's swell
in the belly of the beast.
She said, "Remember, Michele,
if it's worth doing,
it's worth doing well."

That's how she was,
in death, the same,
refusing to give in,
disdaining tame
standing firm despite the cost.

So in these times of decay
when it's hard to see the light of day
not to mention victory,
may their spirits abide,
always soar free
and not be lost
to his-story.

II.

branches spread out over the sea

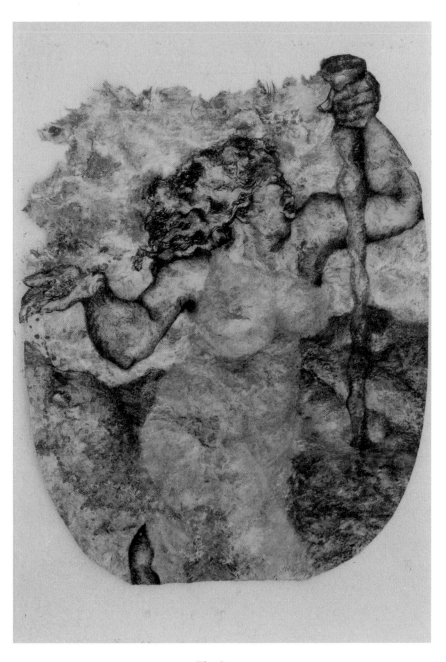

The Sower

1980: wey down dey

when the cab driver
i'd never seen before
hailed me
and said he knew I was a Gibbs
'cause he could tell by lookin',
i knew i was home,
wey down dey.

and when the P.M.,
a blood my age,
said, "Call me Maurice.
We have plenty for you to do.
Let me show you."
i say, "Yes, me brother,"
wey down dey.

and in the ghetto
by the wharf
the beat is Marley
wey down dey.

and de yout' dem workin'
wey down dey.
and de sun is shinin'
wey down dey.

the wind is blowin';
the revo., growin'
and me? I goin'
wey
down
dey.

foreign exchange

It was his first time in these parts.
He had come in from the cold.

"No matter how poor,"
he said, astounded,
"something is always planted,
and grows."

Then went on
to marvel at immortelles
sending forth their flaming blossoms
to daze the eye,
frangipani
perfuming the midnight sky,
breadfruit, fig, and pear trees
he'd never seen so high.

But when those inside the wooden shacks
shook themselves,
unburdened their backs,
began to decorate their walls
with scarlet discs
signifying
the rising of the sun
and with great care
spelled our the people's power
they had won
he felt attacked,
couldn't fathom what they had done.

He wanted the landscape.
They wanted the land.
He was happy to float.
They had taken a stand.

He wouldn't read
the words I showed him,
the letter
written in his own hand,
refused to fully understand

how surely
as the sea flows,
no matter how poor,
something is always planted,
and grows.

pride of bearing

We women walk
bodies balancing
each day's measure
of history's weight.

Belly's birth
toil's triumph
the fruits of our labor
early and late.

On hips
in hands
on heads held high,
each one's load
determines her stride,
paces her future,
becomes her pride:

yesterday's pressure
the new day's guide.

freedom feeling

freedom
is in the spine,
the set of head
shoulders
body-line.

beyond the laws
that pass,
change
with the prevailing winds
of power,
freedom
is in the spine.

the way the children
laugh, run,
tumble without fear—
the helping hands
that set them right,
the dancing force
that guides us through the night.

freedom
is in the eye
fighting
to sight
the rising sun.

a singular compact
with the new day's dawning
that no uniform
code
or contract
can contain or contradict.

a commitment to the future
and the sanctity
of every moment
made inviolate
by how we move
through that space called time.

freedom
is in the spine.

it's simple, but not easy

you can't get out
what you don't put in.

each one,
teach one.

idle hands
+
idle lands
———
———

more jobs.
more food.

The arithmetic of justice.
The equation of participation.
The multiplication of mobilization.
The calculus, in sweat,
of transformation.

Say it any way you like.
This is a working revolution.

day by day

In the fullness of time
the hollow of a hand
the pull of sand
in an hour-glass
following
gravity's natural flow
changes grow.

That pace flowers know
in their unfolding
is mirrored
in this people
molding their tomorrow.

From broken promises
of the past
people learn that surety
is found only
in their own firm grasp
of power,
that nothing,
even freedom,
lasts
without constant tending.

Day by day,
doubt's anansi
must be swept from dusty corners
to freshen the house of the soul,
polishing resolve
'til it glows,
a beacon for the region
which has known so much corruption,
a coercive night
confounding dawn 'til now.

In this spring cleaning
mothers crochet new meaning
from threads
of shed servitude.
Their sons and daughters,
proudly obedient,
absorb this ingredient
and with their youth
weave yet another generation's truth
into life's garment,
firming freedom's warp and woof—
never resting
always testing
how it wears
through use.

If trouble go come,
it have to come an' meet me right inside here.
—Merle Collins
Angel

for the record:

In October, 1983, after four and a half years of peaceful progress in creating a people's democracy and self-sufficient economy, despite constant acts of destabilization by U.S. covert operations, the Grenadian revolution was violently cut short.

Internal division, resulting in the arrest and murder of the Prime Minister, Maurice Bishop, and many leading government figures including Jacqueline Creft, Minister of Education, plunged the country into chaos.

At this point the U.S. overrode an OECS (Organization of Eastern Carribean States) vote in favor of economic sanctions, and chose to invade.

The following narrative chronicles my experiences during those turbulent days.—M. G.

fragmentation bomb: scenes from a war

I

10/19/83: internal hemorrhage

Under a blood-clot moon
the air was weeping night-blooming jasmine
in the garden of my yard
when the heavy-handed youths
obeying orders
came at midnight
of the day
they killed you, Maurice,
to come for me.

When I took it calmly
they saw it as a sign
that they were right,
said,
"Look like you expecting us."
"Expecting you?"
I turned away.
"I expecting anything
after today."

II

The yard of the prison
at Richmond Hill
is filled with light
and the wails of women
brought here in the night.

"Lawwd—
dey tek me
mek me
leave me chirren
bawlin';
in de road—"

"Eh, eh,
what shame is dis?
I fifty-two, you know,
an' to come to dis—
like all de country
lock up, lock up
an' who not,
dead."

And there are those like me
who, quietly,
feel our bleeding internally
yet need to probe
and can't help asking
"Were you at the fort?"
"Did you see?"
"Did word get out?"
"How you reach?"
or saying out loud: "They turned the tanks on us" and
"Yes, they murder Jackie, too,
the beasts."

Peggy's cousin
and Karen's husband
all our brothers—
where were they now?

And the tears flowin'
and the blood boilin'
and the heart achin'
and the mind racin'
back
over the last four and more years
of blood, sweat, struggle,
creation and tears
and our throats well up
to join the refrain

"Lawwd
dat it should come to dis
again."

III

Released from prison
back at me yard
no time to give thanks
or let down we guard in mourning
as the region's radio broadcasts the warning
that U.S. warships
are on the horizon.

Internal division
bloody though brief
provide the vultures with ready carrion
the betrayal and grief
of a people
to fatten on.

They strike on the 25th at dawn
anansi net drawn tight
in imperial design.
Radio Free Grenada calls on the people to fight
so we stand our ground
and block the road
refuse to be goaded into a defeat
that bleats for salvation
by a fleet of vultures
who scorn our rights, our dreams, our culture.

IV

October 25th: feel the weight

Anthony
I see your face
as you came to us
in the first break of the bombing.
9 people and a dog
huddled in a 9 x 12 space
built into the hill
above the beach
you were sworn to defend.

A patriot
20 years old
and an officer in the P.R.A.
proudly you told us
from up Birchgrove way.
And as we sat
considering
whether to stay in the line of fire
or take to the mountains
your smile
broke through the surrounding smoke
as you said
"Don' feel no pressure
all you safe.
Dey go feel de weight
of de revo."

Several bombing raids later on
communications cut
and leaders gone
when you returned for water,
cigarettes for your men,
with news of how the fighting went
we grasped each other
and gave thanks:
you for our spirit
we for yours
battered
but
not yet spent.

The next day it was the same
and when night came
bringing with it
before our eyes
a
u.
s. chopper
downed in flame
i saw again your smile
spoke your name
and said,
"Yes, man,
make them feel the weight."

For two weeks the battle raged
to the dismay of invaders
who had predicted two days
and when, at last,
occupation gained
their lies told
of "only token Grenadian resistance"
i held in my heart
your smiling eyes
insistent that
come what will
dey go feel de weight.

V

And then, the occupation.

"Come out!" they shout.
"Come out and you won't get hurt."
"Out where?" I want to know
being already in the little left
after the bombing
of my home.

And am i some dog
that anonymous marauders
bark for in the road?

But what do invaders know?

VI

In the days that follow
I am with L. B.
bereaved
her lover dead
from tank shot at the fort
named for we fallen leader's
fallen father Bishop
leaving us cut short.
What do we lean on for support now
but each other?

Soon we are joined
by Salwa, Judah, and Rose
blasted by the bombing
from their home.

The five of us sit close
taking solace in each other
and the sound of
"starting all over again
is gonna be rough,
so tough,
but we gonna make it."
And Judy Mowatt praying for all o'we
"Let the sisters walk with thee."

Below the invaders are taking showers
at the standpipe, it seems, for hours
with the sea not six feet away
wasting water
killing time
as children, docile,
wait in line
with their cups, pails, jars
for a likkle liquid
to help them swallow
the barbed brine
of their new confinement.

From our vantage point above
our voices hover
then break out
to shout with power
a verse and chorus of "Buffalo Soldier."
Resistance isn't easy
in this hour of our desolation
our dislocation
the desecration
of a nation's finest flowers.

Even so
we can't play dumb.

When we can't sing
we whistle.

When whistling wanes
we hummmmm.

The jail's been bombed
all drumming banned
and beasts roam freely through the land
recruiting, informing
in a parody of valor
all in the service
of the Yankee dollar.

VII

We don't sleep now
have trouble eating
greeting each day with more than weeping
seeking to keep the flame alive.

But after bad
is worse
and after worse
worser
and after worser
worserer
pli mal
with no end in sight.

By the end of a month
they couldn't hush the humming
so they locked up some
and sent more running.
Those like me with foreign passports
were flown out
by military transport.
Not 'rescued'
we were rousted out
made deportees:

another 'stunning victory'
in their version of history.

But we not dead yet
and it just may be
that the roots we sank
can still feed the tree
however many branches are lost
through the hurricanes of war
and the Northern frost.

We
strong and loving
are still evolving
and will rise above all imperial shoving
inna time.

transition stance

after twisting oneself
into the shape events demand
and rising
wracked
from a wreckage of torn ties,
after facing
that our best
is not yet good enough
and granting the grace
that letting go provides
i come to rest
on another foreign shore
treasuring silence
moving slow
learning anew
the patterns of time's tides
the patience of fishermen
mending nets in the sun
so that when
one sets sail again, casting wide,
the nourishment we seek will not elude us
the song we sing
not be drowned in bloody cries.

roadmarch 2000

Grenada modernize now.
You could dead faster.
With traffic light
but no lane in sight
is serious bacchanal bounce.
Pace pick up in town;
local jetty and board house fall down.
In de wake of de Northern wind,
private beach is renamed 'Pink Gin'
'cause Grenada modernize.

Grenada modernize now.
Bulldozer replace plow.
Foreign exchange
de main occupation.
South end of i'land
planted in concrete:
Off-shore system dig in.
Service to dem
de name o' de game
so forget all notion of nation.

Grenada modernize now.
It go global.
People come in ship big like fort
paying for pleasure
picking dey spot;
ignorant of
Fedon, Marryshow,
and the many who came after
who tried, died, and fought
for what dese new ones just bought.
Grenada modernize.

Grenada modernize now.
Like it skip over Federation.
You could hear German in street
before Papiamento.

De future came toward we
and landed, BODOUM.
But, how to dance
to dis Babylon tune?
Is for we to improvise.
Grenada modernize.

Grenada, after all

when our warring and weeping seem done
time returns us
to this place
where once we felt the embrace
of home.
now, arms still open wide.
those alive and free, full-grown then,
remain unchanged / just more so
while de youth know me,
before i, dem.
through harmattan haze
days dawn clear
though haunted by a pain
no smile can take away.
every gap, each trace
echoes thick.
for every person dey
we feel de weight of how many gone.
history's reefs
crashing too near
to please either visitor or citizen
can only provoke emotion
threatening hard-won surface calm.
for now hold on to dis:
wha' we cahn forget, let rest.
wha' we wahn remember,
light ah ember in de heart,
and wait.

III.

leaves returned to the source

Untitled

taken

I

taken unawares
i feel your welcome
rolling toward me
rivering down the miles
winding willowy homeward
drawing me on.

insisting on our connection
this city
a speak-easy after-hours seductress
opening to me
cares not where i've been
just that we're together again
that i remembered where i could come
anytime
and my arrival coax a grin
from the denizens
who be knowin' all along
no matter how grim life be
on the out side
we be tight
on the in.

II

yeah, I'm back
with my sack of dreams
ready to waylay you
with another tale
of how we be
in far-flung ports.

coursing memory's maze
to pierce the haze
obscuring this river's horizon
i conjure up cowrie, calabash,
clink and clash of silver cymbals
chiming
Yemanja's chorus of voices
carried on the fluted wind
from Accompong song of our elders
to wing on the swift's beat
across continents
to yet another coastal outpost
we try to make the most of.

we meet in full flight
on familiar ground
hugging accustomed curves
with practiced ease.

God knows
what we see in each other.

your body
is pitted, rutted, burnt, scarred, tarred:
name it ugly,
it's been done
and then some.

and i've seen better days, myself,
it's true

many of them
with you.

but girl,
as cities go, you'll do.

and of a night
when lights glow yellow
mirroring
the burnished horn's inner ring

all i want
is for us to duet
in the hold
of that old feeling made new

'cause i been lovin' you too long
to stop it now.

so
let's have one more night out
accountable only
for continuing this affair of the heart
started way back
when even you
were young.

back to the bottom

Strange
having been away
after many years out
sad
returning to continued drought
to see old friends
features all a-pout amid the folds of flab
others dead or faded to a shade.
Buildings
gutted
and hanging
like their gritty dwellers
on determination
and a thin wire
prey to every twist of the wind
in thunderstorm season.

This time
air
on what locals call clear days
had me sick each morning for three months
body rejecting this pregnancy
of accommodation to pollution.

Is there a doctor in the house?

And whose house could this be
So scabby with neglect?
Only an absentee landlord
hoarding the take
could make any sense out of this
or profit from keeping it so.

Is there no cure we can effect?
Or are we so infected
that beggary becomes us?

We skate
on a thin crust.
Trust evaporates in the dust
of another demolition.
Cracks widen
pustules bubble
corruption crests in all quarters.
But yet and still, this period will
have its survivors.

Surveying the wreckage,
shell-shocked victims
of a war which won't stop
search garbage cans
for something resembling a life
that slipped through their stiff fingers
long ago
while others dance,
demented,
down gutted trails
left by bulldozers
cutting their teeth for the umpteenth time
on the land
leaving rubble
where neighborhoods used to be.

In the gray of a September morning
already thick with chicken grease
and diesel fuel
an old woman rises
on swollen legs
from the doorway where she spent the night,
straightening what is left
of skirt, wig, will to walk on.

Yes, there will be survivors.
People who have gotten used to living
with no love
no light
no rights worth speaking of,

pure grit alone taking them
from here to there—
the next stop still
in the middle of nowhere.
They are the one time-bomb
Amerika spends nothing on.

When the fuse of their patience
finally burns
down to the nub
of nothing left to lose
and their blues tune turns hot—

When the tight tether breaks
and their street-corner stagger,
swagger, and sway
becomes a march
pointing the way—
that's a day
to do more
than pray for.

message from the meridian

You came to the right place.
It's just that ironweed and roses
bloom here now
the people having gone to seed.

Upturned earth
manured by passing curs
sprouts purple petals
growing in rhythm
to the devastation
of the wrecker's sweep.

Paradise Valley, this once was
where Black life hummed
flashing hues
flowers only dreamed of
swaying in the wind
of the sweetest horns outside heaven. . . .

But that was then
when Black Bottom was a dance
and living
still held out a chance for change.
Ask anyone.
If you can find them
and they can speak.
Or failing that
pick a bouquet.
Carry it as a reminder
of lives lost, stolen, stray,
but maintaining their color
come what may.
Plant these flowers
and when someone asks,
"What are they?"
say,
"They only look like weeds.
In fact, they are the generation of tomorrow
growing in my garden
and they will not
be uprooted
again. . . ."

Because back in this home-grown groove
being turned to rut
by powers that want it so,
we say no.
Who can't believe in it
should leave it alone.
We don't want
no historical markers designating graves
our ground
paved and replaced by parking lots
where no roses grow.

Even weeds gone to seed
breed trees
casting cool shade
to shelter weary souls.

The cracks
in sidewalks, walls, roofs, smoke-stacks,
have broken too many backs already
for we to be saying 'yes'
to the latest attack
on our territory.
The helicopters
are now steady landing
on the miracle
of so many still standing.
But we,
veterans of domestic and foreign wars,
don't need no more walls
in our Valley
don't want our backyards
turned to alley
will not be roped in
by yet another soldier
proclaiming:
"We destroyed the village to save it."
Mother wit won't allow it
and we who live here
avow it for true:

This Valley
become the Bottom
Black and blue
will be Paradise again
no matter who,
with whatever 'new'
thinks they have the right
to come through.

boot-black blood-clot blues

" . . . It was a day like all days,
filled with those events . . ."
when the official record read:
"Subject appears oblivious to pain."

and when we sang in our chains like the sea
the slave ledger said,
"Subject appears oblivious to pain."

and when they said, "Eat shit,"
and we did
and turned it into fertilizer for farms
their conclusion was the same:
S.A.O.T.P.

in how many joblines, breadlines,
souplines, stamplines waiting,
waiting our turn
did the subjects appear oblivious to pain?

in how many back alleys, open fields, dark parks
did our bodies crumble, separate, flake
from the tar, feathers, knife, rifle, rope and flame
while they portrayed us as the beasts,
oblivious to pain.

in how many sit-ins, lock-outs,
knock-down, drag-out confrontations,
mutilations,
did we hold our peace
while the State rained down blows,
the bombs exploded, the cattle prods goaded,
and the sheriff crowed:
"The subject appears oblivious to pain."

and when King was killed in Memphis
and rage poured forth from coast to coast
across the plains,
the aftermath was "benign neglect":
S.A.O.T.P. again.

and it is not 1865, or 1965, or 1968
but 1991 in L.A.
and you are there,
and after the third stun-gun probe
protruded from Rodney King's body
and they continued to beat him with clubs,
the police account read:
"The subject appeared oblivious to pain."

And a year later
after the four white cops were acquitted
and the jury of Rodney King's peers went out
erupting in a human earthquake
sending all of California up in righteous flame
they still claim
the subject appears oblivious to pain.

This is not an easy story to tell.
This is not an easy reality to live.
This is not an easy time to survive.

And is it Frederick, coming through the smoke,
back ripped open from the whip and rope,
looking for the Union lines?
or Eleanor Bumpers, Amadou Diallo,
Patrick Dorismond, Malcolm X,
Emiliano Zapata, Digna Ochoa,
Maurice Bishop, Jacqueline Creft—
victims of malicious deadly force—
or my sister Edna's son, Che,
in Detroit in this century
felled by a case of mistaken identity
seeking sanctuary
at his own front door
but no

for there are no Union lines
there are no safe houses
no clear sky
or stars to steer by
no leader, either
only cinders smoldering
pain congealing

around the jagged two-edged sword
of our citizenship
raking up a rough and guttered
row to hoe—

no ploughshares in sight
not even a roof—
jails and streets
be all that's full this fall.

so,
don't talk about
what 'appears' to be pain,
'cause who feels it, knows it, y'all

and the strain plainly shows
as our feelings explode
in all lands that prefer
our blood to our brains,
that maintain we are beasts
and treat us the same,
whose rulers bring us repeatedly
to the brink of extinction,
denying the truth
at the heart of our patience:

their way can't last
is going down fast;

and, finally, a small consolation:

there are more o' we
than them.

help

i
always like
sittin' with the help.
you learn more that way.
and get some.
help, that is.
for whatever ails you
fails you
gives you heartburn
they got the remedy
and ready with it.
naming the pain and the craving
'fore you know it
serving it up succulent
with a salivating sauce
'fore you even get
to read the menu.

that's why
they be called 'help':
'cause they can
and do

whoever say
they hard to find
ain't lookin'.

today

today
a
horn's mute
mellows memory
to yellow ochre tones
of autumn harvest leavings
necessary departures
for distant commitments
the grip of October
in the wind-driven city
the dark indifference
these concrete caves
extend to citizens seeking rest.

this year
Motown's ragtime
pounded out by legless vets
patrolling corners
in heavy metal for life
has a muffled scream in the reverb
the bass
tearing holes in your heart.

yes
i've started this love song once more
my wave
licking your shore
my throat
cleared
to explore full throttle
the deepest ghetto gutturals
our survival spawns
the scabby armor of hurt hearts
the corner of hope
still alive

in the guise of fresh jive
my feet trodding true
to the marrow
of your nam
to the zygote
of resistance
in your blood.

so, embrace me again
let me know i'm home.
knock me up
with a future of our own

spare parts

I

the surface is rubble:
pieces of cement, metal, glass,
radioactive trash,
before we even get to ground.
rags, rubber, plastic
prophylactic life forms.
beneath these,
bones.
we are no longer
surprised by the bones
surfacing through the starved-out skin
of this town.
rather,
greet them as the only real remnant
of what was once a village
a people
who came from spare parts
and became them:
forgotten, junked
in preference for the new
rusted in a corner
silent
until a random kick
cascades them clattering into view:
relics of a ruined whole.

II

in this wildlife sanctuary
post-insurrection
30-odd years after '67
the trees are scarred
but the collards ain't bothered.
at ground-level things grow
bushing out
throwing roots
sidewalking intrepid out the cracks

to make unwary visitors stumble
bramble-trapped
in second-growth bracken
abandoned car parts
covering burnt shacks.

the native species swing
from poles
not slowed
by the holes surrounding them.
quick foragers
they go finicky
through what the trash contains today
trained on the crust
keeping them from extinction.

the cold won't kill them
neither heat.
beating all odds
they be on the attack
retreat unknown to those
born at the river's back.

when your head's too hard to crack
all you need
is an equal
willing to meet you
on home ground.

absent that
our flights reduce to fluttering
re-beating Bird's blues
against fences
blood-encrusted from old rebellions
not yet vindicated
barbed wire coiled high
with we inside it
peering through.

III

butt up
at alley's end
a crowd
crouched close
around a flying figure
make a hot compost.
a sound
of skin on skin
hitting
a ham-bone riddim out
insistent smack
met by voices
rising in a rap
break
and snap a dancer
to attention.
he
is all acrobatic invention
stop-action
reverse
flip / split
straight up comin' at ya
motion of the spirits.
the old ones mount him
splay him
pin him, play him
give him wings,
the ground's broken glass
crushed to dust
by this hooved-winged being.

what is he calling up?
what grinding down?
a ritual summoning
alley corridor to tonelle
dancing
the winding trail of memory home
knowing our only way out is in
taken back always
by the sound
of skin on skin.

someday

Someday
i'll write
my last Detroit poem—

when the echoes of Malcolm
at Greater King Solomon
no longer move in the air

when the last
full flattened fifth,
swallowed straight
down the last throat
open to the blue note of survival
rings no more

when Black Bottom
becomes Paradise again—
maybe then.

when the last stricken mother
is done washing
the blood of her children
from the ground where they have fallen
with her tears
and a rainbow appears

when the real criminals are caught
and the beast of greed
born of spiritual need
be laid to rest
instead of the next of kin—
maybe then.

when we finally get the news
'bout how our dues be used
and we refuse
to be abused
anutha' futha'

when a good year
has nuthin' to do with tired rubber

when the hood
is a natural sanctuary again—
maybe then.

when needles
are only used to sew clothes
and we emerge
robed in the whole cloth
of our future—
maybe then.

but that day
is way off
around
a bend in a river
not clogged
with blood, bone,
Michilimackinac's memory mixed with our own,
Tubman's tracks
showing us the way
South this time,
out of this stone cold clime.
Back beyond the way we came.

But as i say,
that day
is way off.

And until then,
while there is witness to bear,
work to share,
and some people to care—
i'll be there.

Twentieth Century Ltd.

in Alabama and Mississippi
they used guns, bombs, prods, and dogs
in Baltimore, clubs and horses
in Detroit, tanks.
and after Newark, L.A., Chicago, D.C.
and every other place post-'68
offered the rank of public office
to a few of dusky hue
who then okay'd
new high-tech guns, bombs, prods, clubs, and tanks
(tethers, too, plus
every other kind of tracking device)
issued to uniformed
and plainclothes practitioners, alike
to keep the ever restless
population quiescent,
cutting short
both fight and flight.
the machines they use to record our votes stay broke.
so, you tell me
what's new?

IV.

where dragons' teeth abound

Blows

blows:
9/11/01

when the bombs drop
does it really matter
how high the tower
or what illusions of righteousness
prompt the hit?

when Philadelphia's black mayor
Wilson Goode
was moved to flatten Osage Ave.
who was the terrorist?

on Hiroshima and Nagasaki
did those blown away
have any say
or were they in any way culpable?
I don't think so.

ask the people of Chile
about 9/11 and Allende.
who was the terrorist there?

and when the U.S. invaded Grenada
because it couldn't control Beirut
were those on the ground consulted?
or merely assaulted and hunted?

yes, let's deplore
all acts of terror;
but be consistent
and careful not to ignore
the arrogance
that makes this U.S. empire
the least defensible
site of all.

911

sobered
by the devastation
surrounding us
on a daily basis
puts the World Trade Towers
and Pentagon guerrilla hits
in perspective,

I don't say it didn't
get my attention
or further polarize
an untenable situation—
just that here,
in Highland Park/Destroit/Michigan
it's only one step
from the cradle to the grave
for all my kinfolk, anyway:
in case you haven't noticed,
Social Services
leads straight across the parking lot
to the new prison.
On this West Bank
make no mistake:
we
are the Felashas
and the Palestinians.

propers

. . . and while we speak of victims,
Bag Mary be missin', too.
you know her.
she was always there
with her shopping cart
and coat of many colors,
faithful
on her spot.
let's take up a collection
in her memory.

She and hers,
homeless before the WTT blast
were also smashed
when that house of straw melted—
leveled
along with those
who passed her going up,
every day,
on their way,
they thought,
to safety.

Who will call for change now?
And who will have some to give?

In whose shoes
do you live?

weather report 2003

phase one

Early March,
weather blustery.
Report from de Nawth:
war, an immanent necessity.
Hell has frozen over,
at least, Hell, Michigan.
in a time of planting
only swords are sprouting.

Saddam Hussein is disarming
but it doesn't matter.
poised to attack Iraq
U.S. troops smack their lips
on cordon bleu and kielbasa
followed by pink Cadillacs
stocked with cosmetics.

but it will take more
than Mary Kay
for uniformed wenches
to take the stink
out of dese trenches.

The U.S. says
diplomacy's irrelevant,
the world's opposition
ignored by Amerika's elephant.

"shock and awe" their only strategy,
the "Mother of All Bombs"
their main gift to humanity.

premature ejaculation
the M.O. of dis administration,
it cares nothing
for calm deliberation

the sandstorms have started,
the moon darkens.
the stock market booms
to old war tunes.
an' de poor, everywhere,
prepare
to be pounded
again.

phase two

Dese words walk
over ground paved with skulls.
dese hands sink
into de gore of war.
dese eyes see:
Baghdad sacked/
the Sumerian tablets smashed/
5000 years of cultural creation
looted and burnt/
the devastation of a country
and its patrimony
in de name of whose liberation?

dis heart hurts
for de people
whose needs never come first
in de plans of their rulers.
dis pen protests
that war is the problem;
not the solution.
dis human,
one among millions,
knows what rough beasts
now sit
as heads of state.

phase three

Now that the lid's
been blown off Babylon,
who seek
shall find Shiites.

phase four

more
terror

I would like to be wrong, but . . .

this year
the sirens sound louder/
outblast the saxophones,
signal closed borders.
split ears with their screeching
keeping people
on their last nerve already
cowering
lest their next steps
take them right over the edge
which splinters as we speak
in a city of unnatural disasters
and crumpled futures
where birds
drop dead out de sky
from unknown causes.

In other latitudes
flags of hunger
ride on shoulders
of barefoot and sandaled multitudes
bearing simple hopes,
old dreams held aloft from the dust.

In some towns
there are no men left
and the silence is deafening.
In some countries
there are no towns left,
charred skeletons
of firebombed buildings
marking the path of the conqueror,
going back to sand,
to bush.

In some places
which have become camps
there are no children left,
no healthy births
and even trees cease to seed

An endangered species
allowing its tongue to be cut/
hacked off/
mutilated
by roughshod rulers
pushing their penile rockets
into the center
of the village circle
while we strangle
making them welcome
may not survive
this most recent diseased penetration.

I would like to be wrong.

I would like to be wrong, but . . .
the facts I need
don't seem to be recorded,
or, at least, are in dispute.

Like,
what is the average attention span
of North Americans?
their children?
how do they swallow so many contradictions?
gluttony fattening
on what future slaughters?
how much arsenic
kills more than bacteria
in the water?

Or this:
"At least 1,000 babies are born
in captivity every year in the USA
to mothers shackled
to delivery tables lest they escape,
joining over 200,000 other children
whose mothers are also behind bars."

Joining them where, how, when?
where does the State abduct them?
to date, I don't know
who will care how they grow
or trace their fate.

How many million dead and raped
does it take
to make a holocaust?
or do they just call it
"collateral damage"
and chalk it up to
"acceptable losses"?
what facts count
when assessing a concept like 'progress'?

for a nation in denial
who'd rather not remember or know,
much less be accountable,
the options are minimal.

well?

Sometimes
there are no words.
the ragged edge of worry
cops on the beat
broken treaties
jobless streets
stolen children
trapped screams—
these things creep up on you.

Where madness reigns
in a dry white season
rains death
rains drought
rains destruction
rains desert sands
the ashes of slaughtered
Iraqis, Kurds, Palestinians,
Guatemalan Indians,
Salvadoreans,
just plain citizens,
burnt pits in our retina
igniting a steady fire of pain—
this reign
has no mercy in it.

The Caribbean,
awash with Northers,
its mouth twisted
by the Yank of the rein
in the hand of the rider
astride its back,
de i'lands,
bombarded
by hurricane, by coup,
by cruel plunder
yet and still refuse to go under,

to sink, scrunting
into the static oblivion
of travel paradise
the North intends for them.
Wait.

Wait
for the next incarnation of leadership
Wait
for the second coming of thunder
Wait
for hate to be replaced by a handclasp
Wait
for each other to awake down the chain
Wait
for this reign to really fall.

And all of us?
landless, leaderless,
pent-up frustration
forking our concentration
into lightning flashes
that crack the night sky open
dry-heaving down to cleave trees
but offer no ease
from this trial by fire.

We
who need water
drown
in ever more blood
from this reign,
this rein,
this rain.

V.

on replowed ground

Dos manos tocando

we

we must make the bridge
'cause it is
'round midnight
arch over space on a grace note
to explore the farther shore of our song.
we must make the bridge.

we must mangle language
to suit our lives
cut
to the gut
of argument
up-end
inherited polarities
'til the axis of the world's spin
revolves
to a yet unimagined slant of vision
hinge our hope on creation
celebrate a child's face
thrown back to catch the pouring rain
give thanks
and begin again.

all-timers

all-timers of de radical freedom movement
don't succumb to de usual
mental maladies.
our particular syndrome
be 'strategically suppressed memory.'
we did it to ourselves:
a precautionary act
in case we were caught.
to avoid confession under torture,
stripped and strapped
to needle-point lie detector,
we could honestly say:
"I cannot recall."
because some things remembered
tortured us.
because we never expected
to live through it all

but now,
the next generation in the 'hood
wants to know what we did:
was it good?
where did it go?
could we use it now?
how to start over?

and we,
though many have fallen,
who be still here dig deep,
see what the hamper holds,
piecing we story together,
mending frayed phrases
to hand down freedom's songlines
charting new parts as we go.

through

when a child
I wrote 'human'
and '100 yard dash'
in the space
reserved for 'race.'
of course,
they crossed it out.
and anyway, 'black' was cool.

later,
crossing borders in the 1960s
back to the united snakes,
for nationality
I wrote 'Afro-American.'
that was deleted, too.

now,
a woman of the world
they can call me
what they like
in any forked tongue they choose,
long as they let me through.

Ole. School

I am ole school.
College of Hard Knocks
P.H.B.: Practicing Human Being,
an apprentice
to actual, not virtual, reality
where the core curriculum is
Continue On Regardless.

I am ole school.
Growing up in a southside Chicago
storefront shack
where when lightning struck
and the electric went out
we'd light a candle and say, "Fuck it."
The leak in the roof
filled the bucket
where we could collect the water
for that night's bath.
Ole school.

Where wasting wasn't even in it
and you grow to know
what come out your mouth
your back must stand
and all you can count on
is being black and dead,
at least, so my father said.
Ole school.

Where the only anthem is "Lift Every Voice"
and we pledge a grievance
against the united snakes de Nuestras Americas
and when you achieve, stay alive,
is not you alone,
but the millions
who were never meant to survive
who together with you win the prize.
Ole school.

Where you never graduate,
just initiate and learn from
each new generation
how to give voice
to their situation.
Ole school.

And what's interesting now
is the conditions that produced 'ole school'
are coming round again, full circle.

So, welcome to the class, wherever you at:
on the stoop, in the street,
in the plant, or on line for relief,
in whatever tower, be it blasted or not,
trying to cross borders unarmed without getting shot,
the lesson ain't easy,
but it's all we got:
Speak truth and rights.
Without justice, there's no peace.
The map of our world
has not yet been released.

May the detritus not trip us.

STAY TUNED.

VI.

an' de fruit o' dis tree became me

Madre de hambre

whachusey?

What lilt of language
tilt of tone
twist of tongue
signify
home?

vowels
belched from the bowels of history
released
to the relatively free
movement of air
intone / untie
multiply rippled rings of meaning.

Eh, eh
oonoo, oho, doudou
tout moun
all o' we
itality
ashe
ki bes sa, ese kata?
how much can
dis base bear?
sinta mira
we shall see
a ver
que tipo de semillas
what seeds issue
from dis tree.

Así es

Mi madre me dio un hueso.
My mother gave me a bone.

Meu pai nao tem lucro.
My father made no profit.

Mi amiga es mi testiga.
My friend is my witness.

Eu como sempre, estou comendo.
As always, I am eating.

Iwo ko mo oruku mi.
You do not know my name.

standing my ground

standing ground I call my own
dat claim me long time now
leave im/print
on foot sole
formed to fit firm
between rock crevice
where light break
but no road go.

reaching a clearing
where sea and mountain meet
on glittering black sand beach
close to belly, navel,
waistband, wide girth of earth
completes a circle equatorial,
magnetized parallel concentration,
swell of my tribe's energy
pooled to wade in.

alive
on dis site of memory
African winds fan me
over Atlantic groans and crashes,
traces of Maroon rebellions
in volcanic ashes
infuse we middle passage
while de Eastern crescent Caribbean
cradles whetstones
of a hemisphere:
rugged landfalls
unabashed
by the surrounding vastness
of sea.

leap

thinking
that going
from street to ground
is not that big a leap
shows just how wrong
you can be.

de switch
from street signs
to landmarks
alone
hone different
lenses of perception.
den, dey is de distance question.
ten miles
can be a day trip,
each bump-filled step of it.
an dat bend in de coast
look so close?
when you try to reach
make progress a joke.

same way
a gap
opens a window in time
propelling you how many hundred
years back
when your line first landed here
where trees speak
and rusted shackles
still creak in crumbling stone
foundations visible through canebrakes
flashing their own story
of lashes to the sky.

the only flags with meaning
be tree and bush green
heralds of we growing season.

trumpets
are a shape
golden flowers take.
war
what big fella elements make.
life
what we create
between waking and sleep.
fill full well.
small countered by deep.

dig

in dis culture of coral
submerged, worn down
to reveal it true form
back a yard
life hard
like rock
knotted
like hole in wood
a whorled world
blood clot
bound
by corrugated tin
seaside shack
going slack
in the soughing wind
whe' we
like crab
scrunt for food
scuttle for cover
shun de surf face
scratching at sand
in forage for safe harbor
watch each wave
reshape we shore.

otra onda

mientras
en Mexico
hay una otra onda
another wave
curling blue
flecked black
by swift's winged backbeat
settles
to foam shell pebbled sand
on this land's fringes
ribbed by mangroves
bridging deep interiors
mauve with lilies
maroon with moss
the air breathes loss
sighs
heaves roots to arch the sky
in traceries
thickened by rosebeak,
cormorant, heron, pelican,
Carib, Arawak, Kongo
flap and cry.

or climb up 8000 feet
in the mountains
below the border
forest deep
on the eve
of the christian year 2000
the people sit in circles
consult their oracles
read the stars
sift soil through gnarled fingers
wait for rain
recite a chain of memories
that make child's play
of Christ's travail
retain their hold
on a life
rendering even infants among them
old
austero.

de Chiapas a Guerrero
Chacahua to Chicago
Wall Street to Woodward
Las Negras to NewArk
Palmares to Xalapa
our bones
hold the land in place.
these humangroves
grooved against the groan
of impossible weight
freight our days
contour a gaze
brought face to face
with ancestral remains
of unconquered though dismembered
peoples:
aqui en Nuestras Americas
these waters our tears / esas aguas nuestras lágrimas
this clotted clay our blood / este terreno nuestra sangre
this porous stone our bone / esta piedra nuestro hueso
this exile our home.

but our fires
have not been banked
this dreadhead is not yet dead
this rope of hope
navel string ringing the world
holds
the interwoven strands of our story
told in bold relief
across our backs
scarred lightning paths traveled
to reach this beach.

on the ground

los pobres rurales del mundo
son siempre
are always in all ways
the most grateful
for any likkle ting:
a greeting with good wishes,
"que le vaya bien,"
shade / sombra
to relieve the heat
a perfect papaya
from one's own tree
agua pura
a good laying hen.

fragile pero dura
resolute
on their patch of land
hard-won place
flowering trace
knobbled limbs grappling
with each foul-weather threat
and fair-weather friend
path worn deep
if not smooth
by stubborn insistence
poco a poco
cada dia
claro que si
estamos aqui
trabajando como asi.
is here we mean to stay
still point
in the eye of the storm
taking the measure
of all that swirls force-ripe around
with practiced equanimity
working dese roots daily
pobre pero libre:
poor but free.

y en Cuba

I

en el campo y las calles
dia y noche
constantamente
como los marrones que son
la gente maneja a compensar
por escasez y crea
una vida muy particular
mas Cubana que nunca
en el balance del mar
entre islas de tres lenguajes
con una alma Caribena
por un mundo entero,
sin fronteras.

II

en donde fé es eternal
y
rum heats a closed room
candle flame lights the gloom
shells click
with seeds, medals, stones
son
to call the orisha down
as a feather floats to ground
summon myriad mysteries:
each encounter
stirring the hot
stock of memory,
fissures the skin of modernity,
antiguo
smoking
con Fidelidad.

On the Lam

Wifredo
Wee fredo, nene delgado,
Lam of Shango
African–Chinese hijo de Cuba,
te celebramos.
nacio en el año 1902
abajo de la cana
al mismo tiempo
en que su país gana su independencia:
baby and country
drawing fresh breath together,
rocked in the palm of the Caribbean.
Hijo de Maceo y Marti,
traendo tu propio luz liminal al mundo,
you drew on power lines,
cultas fuerzas,
learned de tu madrina,
La Negra Matonica, Santeria curandera.

Wifredo,
We fredo, con ojos abiertos,
tus imagenes como un combatante
durante la guerra in-civil en Espana
prefigured Picasso's Guernica
y tambien los horrors reales
de este momento.

Ahora,
cien años despues tu naciamiento,
te recordamos.
Lam,
permeable y durable,
inspiranos.
goad us on to the miraculous.
genio de Nuestras Americas,
ride our dreams into reality.
Ven!

live again among us.
you, quien sabia bien
en donde a buscar por esperanza y poder
y regresada—
in the form of your art
and the beat of your heart—
al bosque de tus ancestros.

fragment:
her name is Nubia

imagine her
running toward you
arms outstretched
trying to reach you
be there with her.
imagine the bullet
bursting her breast
first in the line of fire.
feel the impact
see her
bracketed
to barbed wire
try to save her
fail
and be forever changed.

tu sabes?

our understanding idiomatic
vivimos en esperanza
we live in hope
waiting
esperando
por cambio
for change
intercambiando
claiming our permeability
speaking
in mutually broken tongues
sharing
mutually broken bread
mending memories
to thread our bare/ness/cessities
planting ourselves
igualmente
porque tenemos cosas en comun
where our feet sink
into well-turned earth
soiled gladly in its grip
growing rooted again
by penetrating a commonality
born not of inherited circumstance,
but spirit and intelligence:
an achieved reach
across received divides.

patwa

on day, congote
someday, it will happen
did happen
may never happen again.

we talk
in present / past / future.

walk
de same way.

see
de overlay.

mwen wive.

we dey,
vwayaje.

creation chant

catch, if you can,
your own moment,
snatch it
from the dust it becomes
under power's heel.
finger its texture
ridged keloid signature
unique from all others
cherish the grain.
wet it with love.
reclaim the space its knead rising demands,
baked in the flame of pain.
make it a substance of transformation,
hope's loaf well-done:
we one meal.

VII.
blackward glances

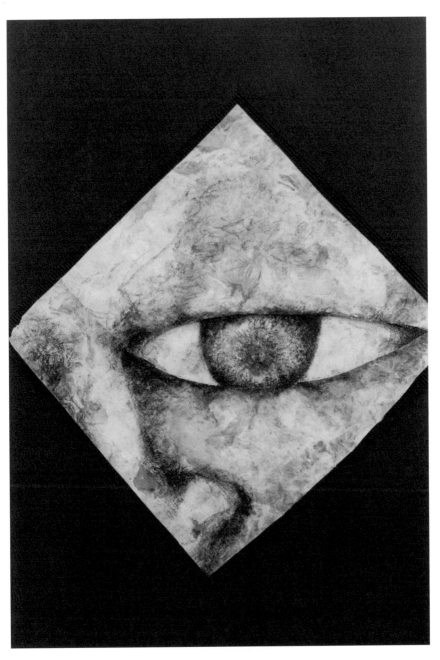

Open Eye

Introduction

Those of us who came of age in the states in the 1960s had among other things the opportunity to be part of a teaching movement from the ground up in the service of freedom. From voter registration drives and freedom schools in Southern counties to storefronts in city slums, we relearned how to use everything, especially ourselves, in order to turn shit into fertilizer one more time. To release the rich loam our overworked soil still turned up and see new shoots rise; to tap the veins of memory and knowledge lying deep in the hearts of the folk to meet the needs at hand.

It was a process that meant breaking down barriers, extending boundaries, and challenging traditional categories and limitations: seeing a world open up beyond the blind alley at the end of the block, the burnt remains of a tree, rope, bones and hope on the edge of town in the dying day. It meant a commitment to change: ways of seeing as well as being in the world. It meant offering ourselves, however imperfect, unworthy, and only partially formed, as instruments of that change. To be leavened by it.

As teachers, it broke down to new versions of HOPSCOTCH for FREE-DOM and "Remember When," "Shine Swam On," and "Rise, Sally Rise." It meant giving equal time and weight to the voices of Carter G. Woodson and that ole woman live on my block. It encompassed the geography of the Triangular Trade, the Underground Railroad, and the safe houses along the way up 'til today: "the map of the world made for our use, not painted the arbitrary colors of scientists, but with the geometry of our shed blood."[1] It meant teaching geometry by mapping short-cuts through ghetto streets and math to manage neighborhood co-ops. Teaching calm in the midst of crisis, discipline under fire. And, as in times of old, we sang.

It was a time when the community was the classroom and history happening at that meeting I'm on my way to now, with you. And when we reached, it meant getting bombed in that church, raided in that storefront office, rounded-up-beaten-and-jailed in that demonstration, shot down in that apartment headquarters, blown apart in that car and killed carrying messages, people, food, books, hope, resources to those in need. And it meant another whole generation surviving those conditions of struggle in the streets and taking the lessons learned there into the established institutions of the country, still mad.

In workplaces of all kinds, but particularly in heavy industry, transportation, utilities, and police forces our organized militancy made the 1970s a time of doing more than speaking truth to power. We were contending for it.

In educational institutions, battle lines were drawn around desegregation, community control of the schools and black studies. With breakfast programs spearheaded by the Black Panther Party, poor children were starting their days with full bellies animating hungry minds. From Watts to Oceanhill-Brownsville,

---

1. Aimé Cesaire, *Notebook of a Return to My Native Land.*

Montgomery to Detroit, and Oak Parks everywhere; from the Ivy League to the cluster of students under the silk cotton tree in the yard down home, a nationwide re-examination of black people's past, present, and future condition and action was going on with an urgency dictated by daily events. Struggles over where to do such work, who controlled that space, and where our true group self-interest lay consumed much of our energy. In the course of this activity some of us placed black women's experience at the core of our vision and the center of our concern. We made it the touchstone by which to measure any movement, time, word, deed, or plan of action. Often we weren't impressed by what was proposed. Sometimes we took matters into our own hands.

As in our lives, our teaching methodology lifted up those voices long ignored or ruled out as authorities to guide our way, the better to explode alien categories of meaning imposed by the dominant culture and to give us language to embrace our collective situation. We even had the nerve to say the living had as much to teach us as the dead, and it was fine to write how we talk and better still to beat out de riddim wi' de drum deh, sar.

Without going into all the trouble that caused, let it simply be said that approaching the reconstruction of a people's memory so they may self-consciously shape their destiny in action, from the point of view of that ole woman on my block, shakes out all the established categories like the moth-eaten contents of a musty trunk in a long-awaited housecleaning. The housecleaning is still commencing. And in airing our story, much is coming to light beneath peeling paint, the distorted intentions of renovators, and the wreckage of years.

In the twenty-five-odd years since these essays were written, the conditions analyzed have only intensified while the necessary work of social transformation remains the same. Yet public discourse has become so flattened and the physical attrition has been so great among those whose work and insights shaped the hopes of that earlier period, that it seems timely to revisit some of these formulations for a new generation thrashing through their own thicket.

The current thicket is heavily thorned with new growths of child and slave-labor in corporate-owned prisons and sweatshops and the hardening of apartheid structures in all aspects of life and thought. These conditions, fueled by the ongoing violent removal of men of color from their communities by the State and by war, the geographic displacement forced upon ever-growing refugee populations, and world-wide corporate poisoning and destruction of the ecological balance create a conflict-driven environment of profound disruption. So profound that the earth itself rebels. And, as we know, the earth too is a black woman. May we heed her rumblings in that form, if no other.

Black-Eyed Blues Connections: From the Inside Out (1978)

Black women's lives are a story about being torn up, ground down, turned around, borne backwards, but blossoming and bearing anyhow. It takes us through four hundred years of shackles and hoes, furrows cut by whips and chains, tar, feathers, and fire. Its warp is Ms's cast-off cloth; its woof is cotton rows; its shuttlecock, neck and knuckle-bones. We can log it by the miles Tubman traveled, the battles Ida Wells fought and lost, the tales Hurston told. We can date it in years, in blood, with pictures: black, white, and colored snapshots. It can have the finish of our choice. We feel it, immediate, when home folk stretch beyond kin; when our kind are called by the bar before the bench to prove maternal prowess to the judge who wants our children put away. We add chapters to history when we live each day, wherever, however, whoever we be.

I am at the Downtown YWCA in Detroit. Rooms on the upper floors are used by Wayne County Community College as learning centers. Since we control no land here, temporary classrooms have to do. The occasion to congregate is always the same: we seek our sovereignty (meaning: freedom, self-determination, liberation, development, power, pride as a people—all of that and more). And, as usual, we are convinced that Knowledge is the Key to the Kingdom. This time the subjects fly under the flag of a Black Studies class for women on Community and Identity. This time the process is called continuing education. At 10 a.m., it is about to begin.

The twenty-two women who appear are all on their way from somewhere to something. This is a breather in their day. They range in age from 19 to 55. They all have been pregnant more than once and have made various decisions about abortion, adoption, monogamy, custody, and sterilization (in fact, every-thing but abstinence). Some are great-grandmothers. A few have their children along. They are a composite of hundreds of Black women I have known and learned from through fifteen years in, around, and in spite of the Movement. This morn-ing we keep on keeping on, with me in the role of teacher.

We have an hour together. The course is a survey. The first topic of conver-sation—among themselves and with me—is what they went through just to make it in the door on time. That in itself becomes a lesson.

We start where they are. We exchange stories of children's clothes ripped or lost, of having to go to school with sons and explain why Che is always late and how he got that funny name anyway, to teachers who shouldn't have to ask and don't really care. They tell of waiting for men to come home from the night shift so they can get the money or car (bread and wheels, dough to roll) for the trip downtown. It can be power failures in the neighborhood, administrative red tape at the college, their own compulsory overtime in the shop. It can be waiting their turn, after others, to eat, or just being tired and needing some sleep. Some of the stories are funny, some sad, some command outrage and praise from the group. It's a familiar and comfortable ritual. It's called testifying.

What is the teacher's job during this? To make the process conscious, the content significant. I want to know how the problems in the stories get resolved, to learn what daily survival wisdom these particular women have. Caring. Not letting it stop at commiseration, I try to help them generalize from the specifics.

I raise issues about who and what they continually have to bump up against on the liferoad they've planned for themselves. We make lists, keeping the scale human. Who are the people that get in the way?

social workers
small-claims court officers
husbands

teachers
cops
kids on the block

I ask: What forces to they represent? Get as much agreement as possible before moving on. Note there is most argument over "husbands" and "kids on the block." Define a task for next meeting. To sharpen their thinking on husbands and kids, have them make three lists. All the positive and negative things they can think of about men, children, and families. Anticipate in advance that they probably won't have the time to write out full lists. But they will think about the question and be ready to respond in class.

Stop short of giving advice. Build confidence in their own ability to make it through whatever morass necessary to be there at 10 a.m. the next day. Make showing up for class a triumph in itself—because it is.

Try to make class meeting a daily activity. Every day during the week. Like language, new ways of seeing and thinking must be reinforced, even if only for half an hour. Otherwise the continuity is lost. The perpetual bombardment of other pressures upsets the rhythm of our movement together.

No matter how much time you take with them, or who you all are, learning will advance quickly when you:

Take One Subject at a Time—but treat it with interdisciplinary depth and scope.

In a variety of ways, the women in class have been speeding. Literally, they will either be on medication, or suffering from chronic hypertension, or be skittish from some street encounter. Encourage them to slow down. This does not mean drift. We experience too much of that already. Have at least three directions in mind for every class session, but let their mood and uppermost concerns determine your choice. They have come to you for help in getting pulled together. The loose ends of their experience jangle discordantly like bracelets from their arms. You must be able to do with subject matter what they want to do with their lives. Get it under control in ways which thrive on complication.

Encourage Storytelling

The oldest form of building historical consciousness in community is storytelling. The transfer of knowledge, skill, and value from one generation to the next, the deliberate accumulation of a people's collective memory has particular significance in diaspora culture. Robbed of all other continuities, prohibited free expression, denied a written history for centuries by white America, Black people have been driven to rely on oral recitation for our sense of the past. Today, however, that tradition is under severe attack. Urban migrations, apartment living, mass media dependency, and the breakup of generational units within the family have corroded our ability to renew community through oral forms. History becomes "what's in the books." Authority depends on academic credentials after one's name or the dollar amount of one's paycheck: the distance one has traveled, rather than the roots one has sunk. Significant categories of time are defined by television's 30-second spots or 30-minute features.

Piecing together our identity and community under these circumstances requires developing each other's powers of memory and concentration. A teacher who asks women in class "Where did you come from?" will get spontaneous answers ranging from "my mama" and "12th Street" to "Texas," "Africa," and "Psych 101." Though they are scattered and don't know what question you are asking, their responses say something about their associational framework. The most important thing about them is their truth. Build on that with the objective of expanding their reference points.

Formalize the process. Begin with bloodlines. Share your own family history and have classmates do the same. Curiosity will provoke diligence, and the abstractions of "identity" and "community" will give way before the faces of ancestry.

Or begin with a photograph from a family album. Have each person bring one in and tell a story about that one picture. Go from there. One eventual outcome of such a project may be to encourage Black women to record these stories in writing, still an intimidating idea. Use a tape recorder to ease the transition.

To help increase their powers of observation and their capacity for identification, have each woman sit in a location of her own choosing for one hour and record what she sees. It can be anywhere: a shopping mall, a beauty shop, a bar, restaurant, park, window. Whatever they feel most natural with. Ride an unfamiliar bus to the end of the line and be alert to the community it attracts. Spend a week riding with domestic workers on suburban express lines. Record the conversations. Help women learn how to use the streets for investigation instead of exhibition. Have them go out in pairs and compare notes, bringing the results back to the group.

Give Political Value to Daily Life

Take aspects of what they already celebrate and enrich its meaning so they see their spontaneous inclinations in a larger way than before. This means they will see themselves with new significance. It also imposes the responsibility of selectivity on the teacher. Embrace that. Apply your own political acumen to the myriad survival mechanisms that colonization and domestication breed into subject peoples. Remind them of the choices they make all the time.

No life-area is too trivial for political analysis. Note that a number of Black women, myself included, have begun choosing long dresses for daily wear. In one class session discussion begins with the remark that we're more "comfortable" in this mode. What does comfort consist of? For me, it means getting past age. For those who are heavy, it means anything that lets you breathe. For working mothers, comfort means "easy to iron." For the budget-conscious, "easy to make." For some of the young women in class, comfort is attached to the hush from brothers they pass on the street. For a Muslim grandmother, this is the garb of cleanliness and modesty. Her daughter, also in the Nation of Islam, gets dressed and feels Africa in every fold. The general principle which emerges is that this particular form of cover allows us greater freedom of expression and movement.

Don't stop here. Go from the body to the head. A casual remark about wearing wigs can (and should) develop into a discussion of Frantz Fanon's essay "Algeria Unveiled" in which he analyzes the role of protective coverings, adornment, and camouflage as tactical survival modes for women in the self-defensive stage of a movement.

Help them recall the stages of consciousness they've all experienced in relation to their own hair. When did they start to regard "straightening" or "doing" hair as "processing" it? When did they stop? Why? If some women in the class still change their hair texture, does that mean their minds are processed too? Read Malcolm on the subject. How do they feel about Alelia Walker in this context—the first Black woman in America to become a millionaire by producing and marketing hair straighteners and skin bleaches. Take them as far as memory and material allow. Normally there will be at least three generations of social experience personally represented in community college classes. Try to work with them all.

Go beyond what is represented in class. Recall all the ways, historically, that Black women in America have used physical disguise for political purposes. Begin with Ellen Craft, escaping from a Georgia plantation in 1848 to Boston, passing as a white man with her husband acting as her servant. Talk about the contradictory impact of miscegenation on our thinking and action. Who do we try to look like now? How? And why? What uniforms do we consciously adopt? Focus on motive as well as image; make intent as important as effect.

Be Able to Speak in Tongues

Idiom, the medium through which ideas are communicated and organic links of association (i.e., community) are established, must be in Black women's own tradition. When Black women "speak," "give a reading," or "sound" a situation, a whole history of using language as a weapon is invoked. Rooted in slave folk wisdom which says: "Don't say no more with your mouth than your back can stand," our vocalizing is directly linked to a willingness to meet hostilities head-on and persevere.

Talking bad. It is still going on? Some class members do it all the time. All of us know women who do. Some with a concern for manners find the activity embarrassing. One woman observes that it's getting harder and harder these days to find targets worthy of such invention. Another, bringing the prior comments together, says there's too little audience for the energy it takes. Whatever our particular attitudes, we all recognize in our combative use of language a pistol-packin' mama, conjure woman, voice of Judgment, and reservoir of ancestral memory—all of which are the bases of a fighting tradition also personified in Harriet Tubman, Marie Leveau, Sojourner Truth, and Ericka Huggins. Discover the continuities in their words, acts, and the deeds done in their name. Emphasize how they transformed personal anger into political weapons, enlarged personal grudges to encompass a people's outrage, got from grief and mourning the strength to live. When words failed, remember how Aunt Jemima's most famous recipe, ground glass plantation pancakes, made the masters choke.

Take the blues. Study it as a coded language of resistance. In response to questions from class members about whether feminism has ever had anything to do with Black women, play Ma Rainey singing "I won't be your dog no more." Remind them of our constant complaints about being treated as "a meal-ticket woman," our frustration at baking powder men losing their risables, and of going hungry for days. Know the ways in which Peaches are Strange Fruit. Introduce them to a Depression Era Bessie Jackson responding humorously, but resolutely, to our options for feeding ourselves when that period's diaspora forced us onto city streets. Bring the idiomatic articulation of Black women's feminism up to date by sharing stories of the first time we all *heard* what Aretha was asking us to THINK about, instead of just dancing to it. Let Esther Phillips speak on how she's JUSTI-FIED and find out if class members feel the same way.

Be able to translate ideological shorthand into terms organic to Black women's popular culture. Let the concept of internationalism be introduced. But approach it from the standpoint of South African Miriam Makeba, Alabama-born Big Mama Thornton, and Caribbean Nina Simone all singing Bob Dylan's "I Shall Be Released." Concentrate the discussion on each woman's roots, her place of origin. Reflect on the history behind the special emphasis each woman gives to phrases such as: "every distance is not near," "I remember every face of every man who put me here," "inside these walls." Ask: What kinds of jails are they in? And what happens when we start acting to effect our own release? Devote one class session to a debate over whether it is an antagonistic contradiction for Black women to use Bob Dylan's music as an expressive vehicle. Explore the limits of national-ism in this way.

Use Everything

Especially use the physical space of the classroom to illustrate the effects of environment on consciousness. The size and design of the desks in our classroom, for example. They are wooden, with one-sided stationary writing arms attached. The embodiment of a poor school. Small. Unyielding. Thirty years old. Most of the Black women are ample-bodied. When the desks were new and built for twelve-year-old seventh-grade bodies, some class members may have sat in them for the first time. Now, sitting there for one hour—not to mention trying to concentrate and work—is a contortionist's or stoic's miracle. It feels like getting left back.

With desks as a starting point for thinking about our youth in school, class members are prompted to recall the mental state such seats encouraged. They cite awkwardness, restlessness, and furtive embarrassment. When they took away our full-top desk with interior compartments, we remember how *exposed* we felt, unable to hide anything: not spitballs, notes, nor scarred knees, prominent between too-short, hand-me-down dresses and scuffed shoes. We remember the belligerence which was all the protection we were allowed.

We talk about all the unnecessary but deliberate ways the educational process is made uncomfortable for the poor. Most women in class hate to read aloud. So we relive how they were taught to read, the pain involved in individual, stand-up recitation. The foil one was for a teacher's scapegoating ridicule. The peer pressure to make mistakes. We look back on how good reading came to mean proper elocution to our teachers: particularly elderly Black spinsters who were also in the church.

We remember that one reason many of us stopped going to school was that it became an invasion of privacy. Not like church, which was only once a week, an event you could get up for. School was every day, among strangers, whether you felt like it or not, even if you ran out of clean clothes for the ritual. Showing up was the hardest part. After that, it was just a series of games.

Then, of course, someone inevitably says, "But here we are, back again." Is that a joke on us? Is it still a game? What are we trying to do differently this time around? To answer those questions, have women devise their own criteria for evaluating the educational process they engage in with you.

Be Concrete

In every way possible, take a materialist approach to the issue of Black women's structural place in America. Focus attention on the building where we be learning our history. Notice who's still scrubbing the floors. In response to class members who pin their hopes for the future on "new careers," pose the following questions:

How is a nurse's aide different from a maid? What physical spaces are the majority of us still locked into as Black women who must take jobs in the subsistence and state sectors of the economy? Do we ever get to do more than clean up other people's messes, be we executive secretaries, social workers, police officers, or wives? Within what confines do we live and work?

Reflect on the culture of the stoop, the storefront, the doorway, the housing project, the roominghouse bathroom, the bank-teller's cage, the corner grocery store, the bus, hotels and motels, school, hospital, and corporate corridors, and waiting rooms everywhere. What constraints do they impose?

If we conclude that most of our lives are spent as social servants and state dependents, what blend of sex, race, and class consciousness does that produce? To cut quickly to the core of unity in experience, read the words of Johnnie Tillmon, founder of NWRO in Watts, 1965:

> I'm a woman. I'm a Black woman. I'm a poor woman. I'm a fat woman. I'm a middle-aged woman. And I'm on welfare.
>
> In this country, if you're any one of those things—poor, Black, fat, female, middle-aged, on welfare—you count less as a human being. If you're all of those things, you don't count at all. Except as a statistic.
>
> I am a statistic. I am 45 years old. I have raised six children. I grew up in Arkansas and I worked there for fifteen years in a laundry, making about $20 or $30 a week, picking cotton of the side for carfare. I moved to California in 1959 and worked in a laundry there for nearly four years. In 1963, I got too sick to work anymore. My husband and I split up. Friends helped me to go on welfare.
>
> They didn't call it welfare. They called it AFDC—Aid to Families with Dependent Children. Each month I get $363 for my kids and me. I pay $128 a month; $30 for utilities, which includes gas, electricity, and water; $120 for food and non-edible household essentials; $50 for school lunches for the three children in junior and senior high school who are not eligible for reduced-cost meal programs. This leaves $5 per person a month for everything else—clothing, shoes, recreation, incidental personal expenses and transportation. This check allows $1 a month for transportation for me but none for my children. That's how we live.
>
> Welfare is all about dependency. It is the most prejudiced institution in this country, even more than marriage, which it tries to imitate.
>
> The truth is that AFDC is like a super-sexist marriage. You trade in a man for the man. But you can't divorce him if he treats you bad. He can divorce you, of course, cut you off any time *he* wants. But in that case, *he* keeps the kids, not you.
>
> *The* man runs everything. In ordinary marriage, sex is supposed to be for your husband. On AFDC, you're not supposed to have any sex at all. You give up control of your own body. It's a condition of aid. You may even have to agree to get your tubes tied so you can never have more children just to avoid being cut off welfare.
>
> *The* man, the welfare system, controls your money. He tells you what to buy, what not to buy, where to buy it, and how much things cost. If things— rent, for instance—really cost more than he says they do, it's just too bad for you. You've just got to make your money stretch.

The man can break into your home any time he wants to and poke
into your things. You've got no right to protest. You've got no right to privacy. Like I said, welfare's a super-sexist marriage.

Discuss what it means to live like that. What lines of force and power in
society does it imply? A significant percentage of Black women have had direct
experience with such dependency, either as children or mothers. In discussing
"how it happened to them," all become aware of how every women in class is just
one step away from that bottom line. A separation; a work injury; layoffs; a pro-
longed illness; a child's disability could put them on those rolls. It is a sobering
realization, breaking through some of the superior attitudes even Black women
have internalized about AFDC recipients.

What other work do we do and how does it shape our thinking? Compare
Maggie Holmes, domestic; Alice Washington, shoe factory order-filler; Diane
Wilson, process clerk from Studs Terkel's *Working*. Study what women just like
those in class say about themselves. Although, as with everything, a whole course
could be devoted just to analyzing the content, process, and consciousness of Black
women's jobs, be satisfied in this survey to personify history, so it becomes recog-
nizable and immediate, happening to us every day.

Have a Dream

The conclusion to be drawn from any study of our history in America is
that the balance of power is not on our side, while the burden of justice is. This
can be an overwhelming insight, particularly in times of economic stagnation,
physical deterioration, and organizational confusion. Therefore, it is important to
balance any discussion of the material circumstances of Black women's lives with
some attention to the realm of their dreams.

In all other areas of life, we can talk about struggle, organization, sabotage,
survival, even tactical and strategic victory. However, only in dreams are liberation and judgment at the center of vision. That is where we do all the things that
our awareness demands but our situation does not yet permit. In dreams we seek
the place in the sun that society denies us. And here, as in everything, a con-
tinuum of consciousness will be represented.

At their most fetishistic, Black women's spiritual dreams are embodied in
the culture of numbers, signs, and gambling. In every poor community, holy water, herb, astrology, and dream book shops are for women what poolrooms,
pawnshops, and bars are for men. Places to hang in, hoping for a hit. As Etheridge
Knight has observed in *Black Voices from Prison*, "It is as common to hear a mother
say, 'I gotta get my number in today' with the same concern and sometimes in the
same breathe as she says 'I gotta feed the baby.' . . . In some homes the dream book
is as familiar and treated with as much reverence as the Bible." In many homes,
dream books produce more tangible results.

The most progressive expressions of our dreams, in which mass liberation takes precedence over individual relief and planning replaces luck, are occasionally articulated in literature. Sarah Wright provides such an example in *This Child's Gonna Live*. In that story of a Black family desperately trying to hold on to each other and their territorial birthright in Depression Maryland, the most fundamental religiosity of poor Black people is re-created, its naturalism released. The landscape is made to hold our suffering and signify our fate. Particularly in the person of Mariah Upshur, the faith of the oppressed which helps us to fight on long after a cause seems lost is complemented by a belief that righteousness can make us invincible. Colloquially speaking, all that's needed is for God to send the sufferers a pretty day. Then children will be cured of worms, the land thieves will be driven from the community, the wind will be calm for the oystermen, the newly planted rye will hold, and a future will be possible in a land of "slowing-up roads" and death. That is, if we're deserving. What does 'deserving' mean? Discuss Richard Wright's approach to this subject in *Bright and Morning Star*.

Relate the fundamental hopes and values of Mariah Upshur's dream to other belief systems through which people have been able to attain freedom. Spell out the commonalities in all the liberation struggles in this age which vanquish the moneychangers. Find examples in our own history where beginnings have been made of this kind. Make the Word become flesh, so the new day that's dawning belongs to you and me.

* * * * *

As teachers, we should be able to explore all these things and more without resorting to conventional ideological labels. This is the basic, introductory course. Once the experiential base of the class-in-itself is richly felt and understood, theoretical threads can be woven between W.E.B. DuBois, Zora Neale Hurston, and Frantz Fanon. Then bridges can be built connecting the lives of ghettoized women of every color and nationality. In the third series of courses, great individuals can be put in historical perspective; organized movements can be studied. In the fourth stage, movements themselves may arise. Political possibilities for action then flow from an understanding conditioned by life on the block, but are not bound by it. And the beginnings of a class-for-itself may take shape. But the first step, and the most fundamental, should be the goal of the first course: recognizing *ourselves* in history. And thereby making her/story our/story.

Slave Codes and Liner Notes (1977)

. . . it was either live with music or die with noise, and we chose rather desperately to live.
—Ralph Ellison

What are we studying when we look at black women's experience, once inside the U.S.?

Documents, for sure. Bills of Sale for cargo received. Agricultural production figures for tobacco, cotton, cane sugar, and rice in ten million pound units. The diaries of white women on the subjects of concubinage and household management. The plantation ledgers of their husbands, calculating the dollar discrepancy paid for mulatto vs. full-blooded African children, both bred for comparative advantage on the domestic market.

This range of material yields important insights, primarily having to do with the peculiarly barbaric variable of slavery U.S. settler-culture fostered. Sometimes, in genteel circles, it goes by the name of "breeding." It meant wholesale rape for profit.

There are other dimensions to the story. Other documents: the vivid descriptions black men have left of us escaping bondage, inciting rebellion among field workers, killing overseers, wrecking property, and protecting family. These are legion. Their perspectives are those of husbands, brothers, sons, coworkers, poets, and the collectors of lore. They demonstrate that we did not take rape lying down.

There are the ways others reacted to our being and doing. The stereotypes of the dominant culture that created Aunt Jemima, Saffire, Topsy, Pinky, Farina, and Sweet Thing. The biological metaphors that told us, in no uncertain terms, what kind of animal Anglo-Americans thought us to be. The consequences of those ideas in action: the spits and crossties where we were roasted after the hunt. Our mutilated body parts smoked and sold as trophies.

And again, in rebuttal, there are the works of art, skill, and craft created by us in bondage that give the lie to myths of our primitive savagery and sloth.

But above everything else tower black women's own voices, raised in resistance to death and slavery—of the body and spirit. They cut a record, in continuous performance, expressing the restless movement of a captive people, for whom home is far away and heaven is out of sight. It is an old song with many verses, but just one refrain: freedom.

It starts with the humming which kept alive African rhythms in spite of the lock-step ankle-chains demanded, and the rocking of the slave-ship's hold. It continues in the work shouts that coded our pain. It rose on Sundays and in the nighttime wilderness from which Harriet Tubman signaled us to steal away cause we were so tired o' this mess. And, closer to our own time, it is carried in the music of five women over the last fifty years: Bessie Smith, Bessie Jackson, Billie Holiday, Nina Simone and Esther Phillips.

In helping black women own their past, present, and future, these figures are primary. The content of their message, combined with the form of their delivery, make them so.

Blues, first and last, are a familiar, available idiom for black women, even a staple of life. In the poorest city homes, records or a radio are the second purchase, after a hot plate. Sometimes, before. For the rural and the homeless, songs are always present.

We all know something about blues. Being about us, life is the only training we need to measure their truth. They talk to us, in our own language. They are the expression of a particular social process by which poor black women have commented on all the major theoretical, practical, and political questions facing us and have created a mass audience who listens to what we say, in that form.

Bessie Smith, Bessie Jackson (Lucille Bogan), Billie Holiday, Nina Simone, and Esther Phillips recall the worst aspects of our collective situation and teach how to wring from that the best transformation consciousness can achieve at precise moments in history. They are the bearers of the self-determination tradition in black women's blues. Unsentimental. Historical. Materialist. They are not afraid to name a job a slave, a marriage a meal ticket, and loving a grind. They all recreate our past differently. But each, in her own way and for her own day, travels the road from rape to revolution. Their rendering of that process is high art. The beat they step to goes like this.

Bessie Smith

Bessie Smith grasped daily survival rhythms when times were really hard. She comes to us dressed as a Liberty Belle, uncracked after World War I. Her note was a clear peal, sounding the simple reminder that we were still alive, despite all. While Ma Rainey established that black women were on the loose, traveling, Bessie Smith said we were here to stay.

She began by recognizing the constant chaos of our lives as an uprooted people, at the mercy of forces we couldn't control. And she made a stand.

> *Backwater blues done tole me to pack my things and go*
> *Cause my house fell down, can't live there no more.*
> *Umm-mm, but I can't move no more.*
> *There ain't no place for a poor old girl to go.*

Floods, famine, natural and unnatural disasters are chronicled in songs like "Backwater Blues." Since coming to the Black Belt, we have been through them all. But, yet and still (as a later Simple said) we had not died before our time. We were refusing to be swept away. We were staying put.

Bessie went further. Since the Apocalypse was a condition of everyday life, our resurrection had to be, too. She took our revival rituals out of the church and into the street, enlarged their performance from one day to seven and all night, too. She preached a spiritual lesson, but she took it from the *Blues Book*, chapter nine: "Women must learn how to take their time."

Bessie Smith redefined our time. In a deliberate inversion of the Puritanism of the Protestant ethic, she articulated, as clearly as anyone before or since, how fundamental sexuality was to survival. Where work was often the death of us, sex brought us back to life. It was better than food, and sometimes a necessary substitute.

With her, black women in American culture could no longer just be regarded as sexual objects. She made us sexual subjects, the first step in taking control. She transformed our collective shame at being rape victims, treated like dogs or worse, the meat dogs eat, by emphasizing the value of our allure. In so doing, she humanized sexuality for black women. The importance of this is often lost. During a period when *The Birth of a Nation* was projecting all of us as animalistic and White "Citizens Councils" gathered strength all over the country, Bessie Smith's ability to communicate human emotion in public and make whites and blacks *hear* the humanity was a victory.

Beyond this, Bessie Smith gives us the first post-Emancipation musical portrayals of black women working. In "Washwoman's Blues" (1928), for example, she delineates the difference between washwomen and scullions. This song is a classical lament, in the rhythm of the work being done. She sings:

> All day long I'm slavin, all day long I'm bustin' suds.
> Gee, my hands are tired, washin' out these dirty duds.

Proceeding to describe the volume of the workload she is expected to handle its effects, she says:

> Lord, I do more work than forty-eleven Gold Dust twins
> Got myself a-achin' from my head down to my shins.

Most striking, however, is her image of deliverance:

> Rather be a scullion, cookin' in some white folks' yard.
> I could eat up plenty, wouldn't have to work so hard.

With these words, she reminds us that the old plantation division of labor between domestic workers and house servants persists and that being a house servant is still a privilege.

Most of her comments on domestic economy, however, center on the struggle to construct a relationship of equality in her own house with black men. The battle between the sexes is waged in no uncertain terms in "Yes, Indeed He Do" and "I Used to be Your Sweet Mama." And, in a whole group of songs, including "The Devil's Gonna Get You" and "Pinchbacks, Take Em Away," dating from the early twenties, her advice to women is: "Get a working man when you marry. Cause it takes money to run a business." The most extended treatment of her attitude is to be found in "Get It, Bring It, and Put It Right Here." It speaks for itself:

> I've had a man for fifteen years
> Give him his room and his board.
> Once he was like a Cadillac
> Now he's like an old worn-out Ford.
>
> He never brought me a lousy dime
> And put it in my hand.
> Oh, there'll be some changes from now on
> According to my plan.
>
> He's got to get it, bring it, and put it right here
> Or else he's gonna keep it out there.
> If he must steal it, beg it, borrow it somewhere
> Long as he gets it, I don't care.
>
> I'm tried of buying pork chops to grease his fat lips
> And he'll have to find another place to park his ole hips.
> He's got to get it, bring it, and put it right here
> Or else he's gonna keep it out there.
>
> The bee gets the honey and brings it to the comb
> Else he's kicked out of his home-sweet-home.
> To show you that they brings it watch the dog and the cat
> Everything even brings it, from a mule to a gnat.
>
> The rooster gets the worm and brings it to the hen
> That ought to be a tip to all you no-good men.
> The groundhog even brings it, and puts it in his hole
> So my man has got to bring it, doggone his soul.
>
> He's got to get it, bring it, and put it right here
> Or else he's gonna keep it out there.
> He can steal it, beg it, or borrow it somewhere
> Long as he gets it, chile, I don't care.

Our ability to maintain that level of control was short-lived. Crop failures in the South and the Stock Market Crash in the North drove us and our men out of the house and home. Dispersed in cities, becoming marginal in both mechanized agriculture and manufacturing, barred from the skilled trades, once again our bodies and souls were all we could sell to live. In blues idiom, the reality was expressed like this:

Merchant got half the cotton
Boll Weevil got the rest.
Didn't leave the poor farmer's wife
But one old cotton dress
And it's full of holes; yes it's full of holes.

The service jobs city living brought were humiliating beyond imagination. A familiar figure from this period is Richard Wright's friend who, as an elevator operator, let himself be kicked by white patrons for tips. With Bessie Jackson, however, the bottom line on black women's self-esteem is drawn.

Bessie Jackson

Bessie Jackson goes with us into the marketplace of the Depression and says "no more auction block for me." In her songs, we are shown refusing to prostitute ourselves, no matter how we were forced to work. Negotiating turf and hours. Sitting down. Battling over the conditions of our labor. In "Tricks Ain't Walkin No More," she makes her position clear.

Sometimes I'm up, sometimes I'm down
I cain't make my living around this town
Cause Tricks ain't walkin, Tricks ain't walkin no more.
I got to make my living, don't care where I go.

I need some shoes on my feet, clothes on my back
Got tired of walkin these streets all dressed in black
But Tricks ain't walkin, Tricks ain't walkin no more.
And I see four or five good tricks standin in front of my door.

I got a store on the corner, sellin stuff cheap
I got a market cross the street where I sell my meat
But Tricks ain't walkin, Tricks ain't walkin no more.
And if you think I'm lyin, follow me to my door.

Understanding as she did the market relations of capitalism, Bessie Jackson pictures how we bought as well as sold. Her songs dramatize the situations in which we became traders in the black market, watching the stock in the skin trade rise and fall (as in "Baking Powder Blues"), letting our chances for raising dough ride on a steady roll. She records how, even when powerless, one can transform physically debilitating circumstances into a means of material sustenance, like food. She follows us as with much effort we worked ourselves *up* to the position of Bar-B-Que Bess, who takes pride in saying:

When you come to my house, come down behind the jail
I got a sign on my door, Bar-B-Que for Sale
I'm talkin' bout my Bar-B-Que
The only thing I sell
And if you want my meat, you can come to my house at twelve.

With total candor, she voices what Prof. Howard Stretch Johnson has character-ized as "the pursuit of alternative entrepreneurial modalities by folk barred from mainstreamed society."

Billie Holiday

Billie Holiday broke this pattern. With her, we began to consciously appro-priate the best in white popular culture as a means of elaborating our style. She then went on to mainline the blend.

First, she made urban blues urbane. All-wise. In Cole Porter's "Love for Sale," she let us know she was Bessie Jackson's sister, subject to the same reality; but distinctions between them were developing. We had become fruit instead of meat. A delicacy, to sample. A black woman, yes; and a lady.

From back alley stairs to (Small's) Paradise, we had made the climb. Appe-tizing, young, fresh and still unspoiled, only slightly soiled, she was prepared to sing about it all. And did. She sang: "Let the poets pipe of love, in their childish way./I know every type of love, better far than they." Now the dehumanizing con-text of our wisdom could be embellished, riffed, cultivated and perfumed. It could be sung to strings. In so doing, she represented a black woman who could conquer white men and their music, "Tenderly."

In her most sardonic mood, Billie Holiday enlarged on white fantasies of being a "kep woman" and the self-mutilation that arrangement required, all the while telling us "I was only dreaming." When awake, she knew as well as the rest of us that "God Bless[ed] the Child That's Got His Own."

She coded our pain by lacing it with sweetness, mixing "Fine and Mellow" with "Strange Fruit." On balance, however, she stirred a bitter brew. The silk and satin were only a covering. For her, as for her black audience, depression and war blended together. She sang "I Got a Right to Sing the Blues" and enlarged her personal misery to embrace our collective situation.

By 1941, with the war in Europe in full swing and black soldiers dying to make the world safe for democracy, she let everyone know that Georgia was on her mind. In the stranglings of the period at home, the bulging eyes and twisted mouths, the victim's blood was ours. Unafraid, she voiced the genocidal results: "Black bodies swinging in the Southern breeze;/strange fruit, hanging from the poplar trees." Even the scent of magnolias, sweet and fresh, couldn't hide the smell of burning flesh.

The smoke and the stink thickened over the next twenty years. Billie Holi-day was one of many American casualties. Korea, Vietnam, Sharpeville, rape, lynchings, and Jim Crow law all added fuel to the fire. In spite of the official freeze on information called the Cold War, we heard of how other border skirmishes multiplied, saw the cracks in the walls, and attributed the disturbances, correctly, to volcanic eruptions in the Third World. The conscious musical voice making a bridge for us was Nina Simone.

Nina Simone

In the 1960s, Nina Simone used her music to revive our roots, to internationalize the terms of our self-determination, and to develop the cultural dimension of armed struggle. More than any of her predecessors, she was able to fuse ideology and art. Her perspective was that the whole world was being Africanized and for us to take our place on the stage of history, our awareness had to encompass the world. So, she opened old trade routes and plotted new explorers' maps whose only boundaries were determined by the "geography of our shed blood."

In "Four Women," she told the tale of violations marking our lives in the U.S. With just that one song, she took us all the way back to "Washwoman's Blues," through Tricks, and watered the bitter crop Billie Holiday knew had been sown. In songs like "Seeline Woman," "Sinnerman," "Zungo," "I Put a Spell on you," and "One More Sunday in Savannah," she cultivated our folk memory. She invoked all the weapons we had used in the past to protect ourselves when organization failed: incantation, congregation, conjure, slave religion, dissembling, the appropriation of European and Anglo-American culture. But she put them to use in a situation and at a time when organization was developing and we were contending for power. The historical moment was such that, through her voice, even songs like "I Shall Be Released" took on a meaning relevant to our political struggle. Her most personal melodies (e.g. "When I Was In My Prime" and "Wild Is the Wind") always contained undertones of suppressed rebellion. When she began her crescendo, no one could ignore the dominant theme.

Nina Simone was not the first to be so direct. In the 1930s Bessie Smith could say to the rich:

> While you're living in your mansion
> You don't know what hard times mean
> A workingman's wife is starvin'
> Your wife is livin' like a queen.

The difference was that Bessie Smith concluded this song by pleading with the rich to have mercy on her plight and appealing to their conscience by asking: "If it wasn't for the poor man,/Mr. Rich man, what would you do?" By the 1960s, Nina Simone was taking the offensive. She performed "Old Jim Crow" and "Backlash Blues" to white audiences who knew they were under attack, and to black audiences who were seizing the time. She wrote "show tunes" like "Mississippi, Goddam" and introduced them by saying "the show hadn't been written for them yet." Her voice rang with social judgment and there were no rebuttals when she told white America:

Don't tell me, I'll tell you
Me and my people just about due
I've been there, so I know
Keep on sayin' "Go slow."

Oh, this whole country's full of lies
Y'all gonna die and die like flies
I don't trust you anymore
When you keep saying "Go slow."

But that's just the trouble—too slow
Desegregation, mass participation, unification—too slow
Do things gradually and bring more tragedy.

You don't have to live next to me
Just leave me my equality.
Cause everybody knows about Mississippi, Goddam.

When that message was taken up by the poorest among us, and all the major cities in the U.S. were being shaken by black rebellion, most white folk were either striking back or asking "why?" Nina Simone was answering by performing "Pirate Jenny." She had chosen carefully. She took a song originating in English light opera, adapted by German socialists Bertolt Brecht and Kurt Weil to comment on life in pre-Fascist Germany, and transformed it to apply to the anti-colonial revolutionary spirit growing in the American South, the Caribbean, South Africa, and situations south of every border. This was the coming storm that her prevailing Southerly blew. And, in the midst of it, still smiling, "looking nice with a ribbon in her hair,/but counting the heads as she's making the beds" was Aunt Sarah, Sister Sadie, Pirate Jenny—giving no quarter at the revolutionary moment. The cleaning woman's final task was stripping down the house and everything in it: to fumigate.

All the covers were off now. The last had arisen and was demanding to be first. In 1969, the song that Nina Simone wrote to say it was "Revolution." The last verse went as follows:

Singin' about a Revolution, because we're talkin' about a change.
It's more than just air pollution.
Well, you know, you got to clean your brain.
The only way that we can stand in fact
Is when you get your foot off our back.
Get. Off. Our. Back.

The only issue was how to do it. For that, we needed more than prophetic vision and exhortation.

If the last among us were truly to take command, all the weaknesses that our condition enforced had to be rooted out. The revolutionary process necessitated that people transform themselves as well as the social, economic, and political structures that governed our development. To reach the "new world" toward which Nina Simone directed our gaze, protracted struggles and long marches began. And there was nothing mystical about the trip. One such earthly pilgrim was Esther Phillips.

Esther Phillips

After the high tide of black rebellion, we all suffered in some measure from the system's retaliation. At a personal level, Esther Phillips experienced all the adulteration, dissipated direction, enforced isolation, and confusion that had been injected into the black liberation movement in general. By the 1970s, she and we were trying to regroup. Her journey toward independence, though particularly lonely, had mass dimensions. Her fight was to overcome all the forms of personal decadence this society markets to prolong our slavery. Taking Nina Simone's advice to "Break Down and Let It All Out," her route led through penetration, not transcendence. And she did it alone. As her own deep-sea diver, she plumbed the depths of our degradation before surfacing with a synthesis. When on land, she said, "If it takes me all night long, I gotta keep walkin' 'til my back ain't got no bone."

Nothing was inevitable about the destination. She was always aware that one road would lead her home, and the other would lead far into the night. In songs like "That's All Right With Me," "Home Is Where the Hatred Is," and "Scarred Knees," she records all the ways we have voluntarily made slaves of ourselves. She deals directly with the three worst addictions capitalist social relations have encouraged in us: surrender to men, religion, and hard drugs. And she tells of their effects with the authority her own life provides.

In her middle passage, she rediscovers something of value in herself. "I'm Getting Long Alright," "CC Rider," "Cherry Red," "In the Evenin'," and "Bye-Bye Blackbird" are from this period. She begins to favor traveling music and straightens up off her knees. Musically, her choice of songs reasserts Bessie Smith's demand for domestic equality and Bessie Jackson's fight to establish market value with everyone she meets on the road toward home. In the '70s, the strenuous nature of those battles burned many people out. In political circles, varieties of separatism flourished. Esther Phillips' expression of this mood was "Too Many Roads Between Us" and "Hurtin' House."

Esther Phillips' triumph, however, is contained in "I've Only Known a Stranger," "Justified," "You Could Have Had Me," "Black-Eyed Blues," and "Turn Around, Look at Me." In this group of songs, she reviews her experiences with men and announces she is fed up with the terms of those relationships as they exist in this society. Speaking directly in "You Could Have Had Me," she says: "You could have had me, baby, in 1973./Now I'm older and wiser and you don't look so good to me . . . /It's too late, cause I've lost my appetite." Not a bit apologetic, in "Justified" she says: "My stock of patience done wore too thin/and I don't think that I could go through another funny scene again." She's leaving cause she got "less than she wanted and more than she should." She concludes: "Now, I'm just gonna be me. I've got no ill feelings, cause I know I'm justified."

She can face being alone and will only do what's functional. The only community she seeks lies in the roots of the "Black-Eyed Blues." In this return, the voice that shines through, loud and clear, blends feminism with nationalism in a strong statement of independence. She has gotten all the loads off her back, as Nina Simone counseled, and has taken a stand where she can.

The only remaining task, for her and us, is to accomplish collectively what Bessie Smith, Bessie Jackson, Billie Holiday, and Nina Simone achieved personally. Maybe the music will help. Listen to it. There is no conclusion to this paper. Only the reminder that the beat goes on.

End Notes

we tell the story: *Goree door of no return.* Goree Island, off the coast of Senegal, became the major port of collection and exodus of Africans during the slave trade.

gut-grounded astrology: first signs: *Mary Lou.* Mary Lou Williams (1910–1981), Kansas City born African-American pianist and composer whose career spanned the entire development of jazz in the twentieth century.

1980: wey down dey: On March 13, 1979 I was with Robert Chrisman in the offices of *The Black Scholar* when a call came in saying that a revolution had taken place in Grenada, West Indies. Like many people, I had no idea then how significantly this news would change my life. In the months that followed, I not only educated myself about this development, but through direct contact with the leadership of the New Jewel Movement which had taken power committed myself to helping its maturation in any way I could. This led to my leaving Detroit and living and working in Grenada for the "revo" until it was cut short by coup and invasion.

P.M. Prime Minister (Maurice Bishop of Grenada).

day by day: *anansi.* Folkloric figure of the trickster as spider; common usage in the Yoruba culture of the Black Atlantic.

roadmarch 2000: *Fedon, Marryshow, and the many who came after.* Julian Fedon was the eighteenth century Grenadian leader who mounted a "maroon rebellion" against British rule of the island in 1795. Theophilus Albert Marryshow was a respected nineteenth century Caribbean intellectual who became known as "the father of Caribbean Federation."

Papiamento. Creole language spoken on the islands of the Dutch Antilles: Aruba, Bonaire, St. Martin, and Curacao.

Grenada, after all: *harmattan.* Rain wind from Africa which is a continental part of the globe-encircling 'trade winds.'

taken: *Accompong.* Region in Trelawny Parish, Jamaica, founded during the first Maroon War in 1739 and still the center of both maroon and Rastafarian communities of belief today.

today: *nam.* Character or spirit, from the Akan language of southern Ghana and southeast Ivory Coast.

standing my ground: *maroon.* Collective name applied to those Africans in the Americas and the Caribbean who escaped bondage, the autonomous communities they created, and the living examples they became of successful resistance in the "new world."

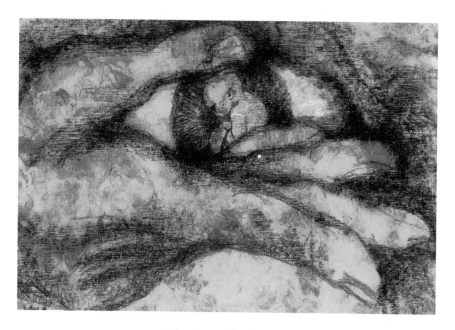

What Future Nestles Here